Also available:

The Commitment of the Lark: poems for looking deeply

Target Practice: a guidebook of 100 poems and one song for your inner journey

Riding into the Storm: returning to face childhood loss and bereavement

Front cover:

The Tyndale Monument, Gloucestershire, UK
Cover design: Rowan Swale
Photos: Pete Armstrong

With particular gratitude to:

Mary Swale, Trevor Blackwell.
Those who took part in the workshops...

Contents

HOW TO WRITE POEMS
FROM A DEEPER PLACE

**meditation
inner work
poetry**

Pete Armstrong

Find out more about Pete Armstrong
and read his blog about the inner journey at
www.holybloke.com

published by holybloke

Conclusion 172

Starting out:
what this book is about

The core message

The core message of this book is very simple. It's in Section 1 ('The Method') but I'll give it to you right here, and right now:

In order to write poetry from deep in your being I invite you to:

- sit in peaceful contemplation
- allow a topic to come up in your mind
- sit with that topic as your object of meditation
- allow words to come up around that topic
- shape those words into a poem
- write it down

That's it. That may be as much as you need. You can go away and just do it. There's no great mystery or great secret about it. Nobody told me about it. I worked it out for myself. You could do the same. Maybe you already have.

So in order to write poems from deeper in your being there's no need to buy this book, or having bought it, to read it all.

Right there is the core, and you're very welcome to it. I don't own it because it's just part of the world and reality. Please, if it's right for you, just take away what I've learned and worked out, and use it as best you can. Explore the extraordinary world of meditation and poetry, and let poems emerge from you to delight, inform, and inspire yourself and those others who read them.

So the purpose of this book is not to teach you a complicated method, because at core the method is not complicated. It's very simple. Like meditation is very simple.

However, if you would like to have someone who:

- supports you while you learn
- encourages you when the going gets a bit tough
- mulls over with you the difficulties and the ways to handle them
- celebrates with you when all goes smoothly
- commiserates with you when nothing happens
- helps you understand the processes behind what's happening so you have more power and choice
- shares with you the really amazing ways in which our creative minds work

then this is the book for you.
Read on.

Who is this book for?

This book is for you if:

- you are interested in writing poetry but don't know about meditation
- you are interested in meditation but don't know about writing poetry
- you both write poetry and practise meditation
- you know nothing about writing poetry or meditation but would like to find out more

This book's intention

I write poetry from a place that is as deep in my being as I can reach, and then share that poetry with others, so that they may be inspired to live their lives as fully as they can.

In this book I'm going to show you how you too can write poetry from as deep in your being as you can, and then communicate that to others.

When you write a poem there are two main criteria that I recommend you use to check it by:

- how accurately does it express the truth of my inner experience?
- how well does it convey this truth to others?

There's also a third, ethical, point that you might want to consider:

- how well does it sit with my values?

So, put aside for the time being what you might have learned in school or creative writing classes about what poetry is supposed to be.

Here we are concerned with the two things that really matter: Is the poem truthful? Does it communicate that truth?

Poetry is a very broad tradition, and within those broad bounds we are free to choose what poetry is going to be about for us. In this book we are choosing to look at poetry as an expression of our deepest truths, and our attempts to communicate that to others.

Previous poetry experience

If you're a complete poetry beginner then welcome! You will bring a freshness of approach and openness of mind that Buddhist meditators, for example, really value. Buddhists call it 'beginner's mind' and they try to cultivate it in themselves because that way the world and all the experiences within it remain fresh, and free of the dullness that habit can bring.

People have come on my workshops never having written a poem in their lives, convinced they couldn't do it, and then surprised themselves. One told me, 'I was trained as a scientist and the whole poetry-writing thing was a complete mystery to me. But you broke it down into its constituent parts and suddenly I understood! I would not have believed I could do it.'

This book will help you understand, and help you, too, to do it.

If you've already got a poetry-writing groove then this approach will be interesting for you.

If you're in a nice productive groove then there may be ways in which you can take what I say and incorporate it into your practice.

But if your groove is really a rut, then you may have to deal with your resistance and inertia in order to help you get yourself out of it. We look at resistance too, in some detail.

Previous meditation experience

If you're a complete meditation beginner then welcome! As with the poetry above, your 'beginner's mind' is an asset that all experienced meditators try to maintain. On retreats, days of mindfulness, and in groups and workshops I have introduced many people to meditation for the first time. I look forward to sharing the joy of meditation with you here in this book. One way of describing meditation is that it is a new way of meeting the world.

If you have existing meditation experience then I think you will find enough in this book to interest you and perhaps influence your practice. Who amongst us can say we know it all?

Inner journey

Writing poetry from deeper in your being is a variation on the theme of inner journey. It is not separate from that journey, because nothing is separate from that journey.

Writing poetry may be a support for that journey. It may become the journey itself. Or it may possibly be a distraction from the journey.

Ultimately it's not the poetry that's important; it's your connection with Reality.

The barriers within

When I contemplated writing this book, amongst the surge of creative energy and ideas and material, I came up again and again against the question: Who am I to write this?

Beyond the barriers of my resistance, I know I have so much to offer. The barriers are what stop me.

This is true for many of us, much of the time. We have to find ways to carry on: ways to undermine, circumvent, overcome or transform the barriers. Under, around, or over the barriers – or transformation of the barriers. We'll come back to this later, because it is a crucial topic.

Two approaches to meditation or inner working

What I'm advocating in this book is an approach to writing poetry that utilises two different approaches to meditation or inner working.

The first is the 'classic' meditation practice, which encourages us to focus on breathing or some similar method in order to enter a clearer inner space, and then recommends that we simply witness what happens. Through this practice we become ever more mindful and aware, ever more in connection with a deeper reality. We are aware of what is happening, while it is happening, whatever it is.

The second is a more active approach to what happens when we enter a clearer inner space. We can use tools and techniques to engage with what is happening within us and tease out meaning and insight from that. This owes more to developments in psychotherapeutic approaches, especially process work. It's a lot of fun!

How this book is organised

Section 1 is 'The Method'. We get straight into working our way through the stages that will best help you write a poem from deep. In this section I take you through the method twice: once in short order, and once in medium detail.

Section 2 is 'The Method' in a lot of detail. It's a comprehensive guide to everything you need in order to write poems from a deeper place. We also answer some of the questions that are likely to come up when you have experience of shaping your own poems in this way.

Section 3 is about 'Barriers: our inner critics, our shadows, and our eccentricities.' It's about all the stuff that will and does get in the way. It's about the difficult areas that prevent us from being in touch with our deeper selves and from shaping poetry. We look at how to recognise those barriers, and how to deal with them.

Section 4 is 'Moving on to a different level.' This looks at questions that may arise when you've been practising the method for some time, and provides additional ways forward for you.

We finish the book in the usual way: with a conclusion!

Section 1 The Method briefly

I'm going to describe the method to you three times.

Firstly, in this section, I'll give you a brief overview so you can get the basic shape clear in your mind. Then I'll give a lengthier list of the various steps in the process. At that point I recommend you try it out for yourself.

In Section 2 I'll go through each of those steps in a lot of detail so you can really get to grips with the ins and outs: all the possibilities as well as the potential difficulties and what to do about them. OK? Ready to go?

A quick overview

In order to write poetry from deep in your being I invite you to:

- sit in peaceful contemplation
- allow a topic to come up in your mind
- sit with that topic as your object of meditation
- allow words to come up around that topic
- shape those words into a poem
- write it down

A few things to notice:

- this is an invitational process, not an exercise in forcing ourselves
- we are moving into our inner world, and then from our inner world back to the outer world, and translating from the non-verbal to the verbal along the way

- we don't pick up a pen (or a computer keyboard) until right at the end, when the poem is, in effect, already written

If you want, you can try this process right now. You don't have to read about it anymore, or receive further guidance. Those six points, right there, may be quite enough for you. Please, if it feels right, do go on and use this method to write a poem.

How long does it take? As long as is right! I've worked with groups where we sit for ten minutes, then move into phases 2-6 over the next 30 minutes and get satisfying results. So, forty minutes for the whole thing.

When I'm buzzing with possibilities then the process could take me 15 minutes. When I'm not buzzing, and being a bit rambling and dozy, I might spend two hours or more over it.

However, if you don't feel ready yet it may be wise to wait until you have a better grip on what to do. That way you can feel more confident when you go into experiencing the process for yourself.

A lengthier list of steps

A process like this is like a journey or a spectrum. We can divide it up into any number of different stages. It depends on how detailed we want to be. With our brief overview we had six steps. Now for this lengthier list I'm going to describe eleven steps. Remember that after this we'll look at each step in a lot more detail, so don't worry if not everything makes sense at this time. All (or most) will be revealed…

And just before we go on, a word about 'writing' poems. As we've seen already, the process I describe does involve actual writing, or typing, but that happens quite late in the process. In order to describe this whole process more accurately I often use the phrase 'shaping up poems' – because that's what it feels like. The poems come into a poem-like shape inside us and then we write them down. Sometimes I use the phrase 'writing poetry' to mean the whole process, not just the writing down part. The context should make this clear.

1 Forming an intention

Be clear about what your intention is. This will make it more likely that you will be able to stick with it through the inevitable difficulties and distractions. How you do this is personal to you. You can make up a simple, clear, phrase to say to yourself. For example, 'For the next half hour I will sit quietly and focus on shaping a poem.'

2 Sitting in peaceful contemplation

Find a quiet place where disturbances are at a minimum. Sit in a comfortable pose where you can be relaxed but alert. This is an odd combination, but practice will bring, if not perfection, then at least a greater competence. Close your eyes, focus on your breathing, and notice what happens moment by moment. When you notice that you have drifted 'off' or 'away' then come back to your breathing, come back to yourself in the present moment with good humour and compassion for yourself.

3 Getting clear

When you sit in contemplation for a while you will often (not always!) experience a sense of greater clarity than you are used to in your everyday life. This has been likened, classically, to a glass of cloudy water becoming clearer as the mud or dirt settles down to the bottom. So effectively there is nothing to do to make this happen, apart from wait and allow it to happen. That's actually pretty hard to do sometimes, but that is what is required.

4 Allowing a topic to emerge

Let's assume you've been sitting for a while and you've noticed a greater sense of clarity than you are used to. From within this space you can now range lightly over what you've noticed during this period, or what's happened recently in your life, and from that range allow one topic to emerge that you can focus on. Often this just happens: it's clear to you what that topic is. Sometimes, if it doesn't emerge, then you will need to choose a little more actively. My recommendation here is to choose that subject which has the most energy and feeling for you.

5 Meditating around the topic

Take that topic and treat it as your object of meditation. This means that you hold it in your mind. In the same way that you might focus on your breathing, or a mantra, you focus on your topic. You notice what comes up for you around it. If you drift 'off' you simply return good naturedly to your topic.

6 Allowing words to arise

When the image, or experience, or topic, or event has been in your mind for a while and you have a feel for it, start to allow words to appear around it, and notice what they are. Let words, and phrases, appear, and let them build up and lead to other words and phrases. If a particular pattern starts to feel right, you can stick around that and let it grow.

7 Shaping a form

Gradually allow a sequence, a pattern of words, to form. Then go over your sequence of words in your mind time after time so that it fines down and comes together as a whole. When you do it in your mind in this way then the parts all influence each other and it's easier for it to hang together as a whole.

8 Writing down

At some point when you're ready, or often when you don't feel ready but it's time to do it anyway, write the poem down on the page. Don't fuss too much at this stage. Just get it down as a whole, quickly, while it is still in your mind. You can refine it more when you come to the next stage. If the other parts have worked well it shouldn't take long. This part often takes me no more than ten minutes, sometimes less.

9 Immediate editing

I like to make the original write-down by hand (my typing is none too quick) and then transfer the poem to a laptop a little later with a nice pot of tea. At this stage you can make a few adjustments or amendments to make the poem more truthful, or more comprehensible. There's an important distinction between those kinds of edits and a comprehensive re-write. You're too close to the poem at this stage to know what it truly is, what this new creation really is that you've given life to. You can't know what is 'good' or 'not good'. Trust in the model, trust in your inner process, trust in the poem, and, for a good while, let it be much as it is now.

10 Later editing

After a few days, weeks, or months of maturation and life, come back to the poem and see it with fresh eyes: more as a reader, less as a writer. Maybe make some changes, some improvements. At this stage get a trusted friend or two to read it and give you feedback as to where it works for them or where it's not clear. Make changes as you see fit. Almost always these changes will be relatively minor. We'll look at why wholesale re-writes aren't necessarily for the best later.

11 Sharing

When the time is right, you may wish to let your poem out into the world in some way. Make it available to others, even if only to your future self. Keep it moving!

Before we go on, an invitation

Now at this point you have a choice. With this longer list of steps you have enough information to give the process a go. You may not feel quite ready but who does feel ready when they try something for the first time?

My recommendation is that you read through the simple list and the longer list a couple more times so you have it more clearly in your mind, and then give it a go, maybe even several times.

Don't worry about getting all the details right – they are only guidance. The question is – how does it work for you, and where is it tricky? Does it enable you to shape up a poem?

At this stage don't worry too much, (or even at all) about what comes up for you, and particularly as to whether the poem 'is any good'. That question is usually around, but for the time being ignore it. (Later on we'll look at how to deal with that bad boy properly...).

For the purpose of learning this process I'm going to redefine a poem for you. It is any arrangement of words that has meaning for you. I hope that's broad enough to be reassuring and encouraging at this stage.

The reason for having a go at this point is that the more detailed look at the different stages we're about to go into will make more sense if you've already got some experience. Also, too much detail can be overwhelming at an early stage.

So, please, find yourself a quiet spot, give yourself thirty to forty minutes, and have a go. See what happens! 'Success' at this point comes from trying something new, and learning from whatever happens.

Section 2 Step by step
with lots of detail

The only method that counts is the one that works for you, the one that leads consistently to poems that come into shape from deep in your being, and convey your truth to other people in a way that inspires them. The method that works for you may look, in the end, nothing like my method.

In fact I hope that even if you start with 'my' method you quickly adapt and adopt it into 'your' method – the one that works consistently for you. If or when you do – let me know about it!

Step 1 Form an intention

Sometimes when I sit down to meditate I get lost. I 'wake up' after say fifteen minutes and realise I've just been off with the fairies, fantasising about this, worrying about that, remembering about the other.

I've made the error of assuming that just because I've been meditating for years, I know how to do it and will automatically slot into my usual practice. Not so, my friends, not so. That is a common error and I make it frequently. Our habitual energies and our tendency to prefer a life of ease and comfort are always available to ambush us.

One way to counter this is to be really, overtly, verbally clear on what you intend to do before you sit down. For example, I might say to myself: 'I am now sitting and focusing on my breathing for 20 minutes, and then for a further 30 minutes I am shaping up a poem.'

Or I might say, because I know I'm feeling disturbed and upset by something that happened previously, 'For the next 30 minutes I am going to sit quietly and look deeply at my anger from yesterday. Whenever I find myself drifting off, I will come back to my anger.'

Or I might say, because I have something buzzing in my mind that wants to be expressed, 'I will sit for half an hour and shape up a poem about xxxx.'

Now none of these expressions of intent guarantee that you will actually carry out the intention, but they do make it much more likely.

As part of your intention, it's helpful also to have a clear sense of who you are writing for. Who you are writing for will shape to some degree what you think you can say, and the way you think you can say it.

I look at this subject in more detail in Section 4.

For the time being, if you have no clear audience in mind yet, I recommend either that you imagine you are writing for the person or people you love and trust the most in the world, or that you say to yourself that at this stage you are writing purely for yourself, and only later will you decide whether you will let anyone else in on the results. This is in order to really protect the creative space of vulnerability and truthfulness that you are attempting to enter.

Queries about forming an intention

I've formed my intention but I still drift away.

Another source of support for your intention is to have a word or short phrase to bring you back when you find yourself drifting astray (and you will, because that's simply what happens to everyone). It could just be 'Poem', or 'Shape poem', or 'Deep' for example. It needs to be your word, and it needs to work for you, and what works for you will probably change over time.

Step 2 Sit in peaceful contemplation

I'm going to assume you have no knowledge of meditation or similar practices, and so I'm going to take you through a basic introduction, enough to get you started and going forward.

If you already know about this and practise regularly then you could skip this section. On the other hand (remember 'beginner's mind'?) there's always something new to learn, or some different angle to appreciate, so maybe you should hang on in here.

Here's my invitation to you. Try this:

- Find a quiet place where disturbances are at a minimum
- Sit in a comfortable pose where you can be relaxed but alert
- Close your eyes
- Be aware of your body
- Be aware of your breathing
- Notice what is happening moment by moment
- When you notice that you have drifted 'off' then come back to your breathing with good humour and compassion for yourself

If you're practising this meditation part on its own, then after a period (say 20 minutes) you can bring the meditation to an end, come back to 'normal' life, and review what happened. If you're practising as part of the whole sequence of steps in shaping a poem, then after a period (could be 10-20 minutes) this phase will shift into the next.

More on peaceful contemplation

Let's go through the points above in a little more detail.

Find a quiet place where disturbances are at a minimum

This could be a quiet room in the house: a bedroom, a study. It could be a shed in the garden, or, on a sunny day, the garden itself. Most outer disturbances will come from other people, so if you share your space with others, maybe it's about choosing a time when they are out, or saying to them: I just need this room to myself for an hour. Or: can you be especially quiet around me for the next hour?

Timing may be influenced by other people, but also by your own habits. When is a generally quiet time of day for you? When can your own mind be most easily persuaded to quieten down? For some people (myself included) early in the morning is a good choice. For others, a lunch-time break is good, or later in the evening.

If there is no part of your day that is ever quiet, then consider re-shaping your life a little! However, with the right intention, and a certain amount of concentration and persistence, any time, and any place, is possible and is better than nothing at all.

Sit in a comfortable pose where you can be relaxed but alert

'Comfortable pose' means 'comfortable pose for you'. It's your body, and you will have the best knowledge of what works for you.

For most of us, 'comfortable' will mean sitting on a chair, with support for our backs. This can be an armchair. That's what I often use, and it works for me. I also sit up in bed early in the mornings, propped up on pillows. That also works.

There's sometimes a mystique in meditation circles about sitting poses (lotus position, half lotus…). There can sometimes be a certain pressure to sit on a cushion on the floor, or a subtly competitive element about it. I remain unconvinced that, unless we're young and flexible, deliberately putting ourselves into uncomfortable physical positions, with stress on knees and backs particularly, and holding those positions for a length of time, is the best way to proceed to nirvana.

If you've been training yourself to sit on a cushion on the floor and you're comfortable with it, or if you are young and/or naturally balanced and flexible, and comfortable with a cushion on the floor and no support for your back, then fine!

Other alternatives between armchair and floor cushion include sitting on a straight-backed chair, or kneeling on a little meditation stool. In regular meditation circles there are justifications for the more formal physical postures in terms of benefits for your meditation. However, here we are concerned primarily with poetry, not meditation, so we are freer to pick our own way.

Moving on from poses…
'Relaxed but alert' is a strange combination.

We're used to both states of mind, but separately. When we are relaxed, we just let our mind drift, perhaps on to anything that happens to come up, perhaps into sleep. When we are alert, we tend to be focused on the world around, or on the task in hand.

In 'relaxed but alert' we're looking for a state of balance where our mind is not giving in to anything that comes along, but neither is it actively pursuing a particular line of thought. It's a state of balance that is like riding a bicycle: a little strange when you first try to learn, but once you get the hang of it, you're away!

Another analogy is to say that you are asking (a part of) your mind to be in the role of steward at the entrance to a hall. The job is to stay alert and watch everyone that goes in and out. And that's it. Avoid falling asleep on the job, avoid chatting with your mates, avoid heading off to fix the drains. Just stay there and be alert, and notice what happens.

Close your eyes

For most of us closing our eyes will work fine, most of the time. Some Buddhist traditions recommend eyes open. If that's what you are used to then that's what you could continue with. However that may make it more difficult for you when we come to later stages in the process. At that point having your eyes closed will make it easier to visualise images, or allow words to arise. I'd recommend flexibility here.

Be aware of your breathing, be aware of your body

In order to sit in contemplation, in meditation, I suggested paying attention particularly to your breathing, and to your body. 'Awareness of breathing' is one way to approach meditation. There are others which you may already know, or which may work better for you.

If you do use awareness of breathing, then when you drift 'off,' coming back to your breathing can be a familiar and simple practice that helps you gradually deepen your connection with the moment – with this moment.

Sometimes it is helpful to count your breaths – often in batches of ten – in order to facilitate developing the kind of awareness of breathing that will enable you to enter a clearer space. You can experiment with this. I still do this quite a lot when I first begin to meditate.

Awareness of your body is also a key factor. There's a bit of a paradox here. Understandably we often consider meditation to be a mental process. After all, it's about the mind. Isn't it? Well, no, actually.

The traditions say (based on hundreds of years of experience) that the mind isn't separate from the body – or from our feelings, or from anything. What this means practically is that we can enter the meditation space via our mind, or our breathing, or our body. We can do walking meditation for example. We can do sitting meditation, but concentrate our awareness on our body, going through each part and recognising and appreciating it. This helps us to enter the moment – this moment – more readily.

There is a wealth of experience and knowledge out there to support you if you want to take it further. But in this book, we'll leave it at that for the moment.

Notice what is happening moment by moment

You may begin to notice what is happening with your breathing. Some of the amazing minutiae of your breathing process – you know, that simple in and out of your diaphragm that keeps you alive all your life – may start to become apparent to you.

You may notice aspects of your bodily sensations that you don't normally register: little tics in your face, an ache in your arm, a sense of your heart working away to pump the blood around your body.

You may notice the thoughts, and the patterns of thoughts, in your mind. You may notice feelings arising in response to thoughts, or thoughts arising in response to feelings.

One way to describe the skill you are trying to develop is by calling it 'the witness'. Like the steward in our analogy earlier, you are seeking to remain as a witness to all that arises, without being carried away by it.

When you notice that you have drifted 'off' then come back to your breathing with good humour and compassion for yourself

Drifting away from awareness – awareness of your breathing, of your body, of this moment – is very common. It's so common that I tell people that it is an integral part of the meditation process. It's not that there is meditation – where you are mindfully aware of what is happening while it is happening – and non-meditation, where you have lost connection and drifted away. It is that the meditation process is the whole sequence: being aware, being less aware, drifting off, realising you've drifted off, back to being aware, and so on...

That's the deal. The length of time between instances of losing awareness may get longer as you become more skilled. When you are very experienced they may get very long indeed. But I think the gaps will occasionally still be there.

The key to developing the skill is to treat the whole sequence with warm and affectionate interest. If you can, avoid getting into a strop about it, or getting a sense of disappointment, or failure. If you do get these things, see if you can view them with warm and affectionate interest...

Further study on peaceful contemplation
There are already very many books, courses, workshops and advices on how to meditate. You can't read them all, listen to them all, or implement them all. My suggestion, if you want to go into it further, is that

you treat the whole territory as an action research project. Try different approaches and find what works for you consistently. And then recognise that that too will change over time.

My invitation above is quite good enough to get you started and, hopefully, enjoying what you do. Meditation sometimes has a reputation as a serious, disciplined activity for serious disciplined people. And that's partially true. But also true, and one of the important secrets about meditation is that it can be a whole lot of fun. Meditation is exploration, and exploration is fun. It opens up new territories and that too is fun!

Yes, if you want to become a Zen monk then you will have to sit in meditation for hours every day with your knees twisted into a lotus position and occasionally be beaten with a stick on your shoulders, and that may not always be entirely enjoyable... But luckily all we are interested in here is this: what helps me to shape up poems that express more of my deeper truths than I would otherwise. And for that purpose, a basic ability to sit quietly and contemplate what's happening in your mind and body is all that's really required.

In this book I bring together two approaches to inner work. One is 'classic' meditation, where you sit in quiet contemplation and notice what arises, and let it pass. The other is a more active, therapeutically-based method of working with your inner processes. In this approach there are some great tools available to help generate insights into the nature of your being, and the nature of reality. We look at these in more detail later.

Queries about sitting in contemplation

My mind won't settle; I'm just daydreaming all the time.

Follow your unsettled mind. Be interested in your daydreaming. Watch what happens. Notice if you're developing a 'witness' that can observe whatever is happening while it is happening – that is a skill to celebrate, but like any skill it takes time to learn and develop.

I find it boring.

Get interested in your boredom: what's it like in detail? Where in your body do you feel it? What's that feeling like? How do you know you're bored?

I keep falling asleep.

Try meditating with your eyes open. Some traditions do this as a matter of course. They suggest you keep your gaze on a point a few feet on the ground in front of you. Or face a blank wall.

Or try to enjoy falling asleep, and then enjoy waking up! What is that like for you? What are your attitudes to sleep? Is there some critic inside having a go at you about you not paying attention? Whose is that voice? (We'll deal more fully with the critic in Section 3.)

I keep being distracted by the noises from the street outside.

Try treating them as sound that comes and goes. Be interested in the phenomena of sound – how does that work? What is it you are actually experiencing when you describe it as 'hearing noises from the street'? Try to be aware of them without being sucked into them.

You can also take the noises as your object of meditation. Focus on the noises and when you find yourself drifting 'off' (for example you notice you are focusing on your breathing instead...) then you gently and compassionately bring yourself back to the noises in the street. What you are doing with this process is developing your concentration – your capacity to hold something in your mind over a period of time. It's a skill, it takes time to learn, and the likelihood is that you won't be able to do it effectively straight away.

Birdsong can be a very good focus for meditation practice. It's non-verbal, and usually not melodic, so it's less easy for us to fit it into our normal patterns, switch off, and drift away.

My everyday mind won't go quiet – all that comes up for me is planning and reviewing and worrying at stuff.

This is a common issue. The standard response is to say just keep persisting. Notice your focus on your everyday mind and then, compassionately and good-humouredly, return to your breathing. And indeed often this is sufficient, and you gradually develop that capacity for quiet where your everyday mind takes a rest.

However, sometimes stronger measures are called for. For a deeper understanding and longer-term solution you might have to consider a different kind of approach, and we will look at this in Section 4 – Moving on to a different level.

Step 3 Getting clear

When you sit in contemplation for a while you will often (not always!) experience a sense of greater clarity than you are used to in your everyday life. This has been likened, classically, to a glass of cloudy water becoming clearer as the mud or dirt settles down to the bottom.

If your everyday mind is like my everyday mind (and most other people's everyday minds), then it is busy, busy, busy. If it's not working out plans and projects, or worrying over the past, if it's not dealing with easy or difficult conversations, if it's not trying to remember what it knows it's forgotten, then it is probably 'relaxing' by watching TV, scrolling down on a phone, or doodling around on a computer.

Hmmm. That's busy. That's normal. That's not a great state to try to write a poem from.

Any move along the spectrum towards less busyness and greater stillness and clarity will be an improvement, and make a better environment from which a deep and satisfying poem is more likely to emerge.

When you sit down initially, unless you are a natural, or very lucky, you will find peace difficult to come by. Your everyday mind is used to being busy, and likes, on the whole, to stay busy. Being asked to do, effectively, nothing, is not the huge treat we might expect. Your mind will, out of habit, usually resist the request.

The key is (a) not to have unreal expectations and (b) to be persistent.

Just stay with it, notice what happens, and if you can, enjoy it all. And I mean all: enjoy the non-peace, enjoy the glimpses of clarity, enjoy the peace when it comes, enjoy the change to busyness when it happens (and it will).

There's a strange way in which the more you pursue peace and clarity in an agentic, goal-oriented way, the less likely it is to come to you.

It's like a saying about enlightenment: enlightenment is like an accident; you can't make it happen, but you can make yourself more accident-prone.

Or, as the wise people from the folk say: you can lead a horse to water, but you can't make it drink.

You can't make more peace and clarity happen, but you can create the conditions in which they are much more likely to emerge.

Another analogy is to think in terms of badger–watching. You want to see the badgers? What do you do? You put yourself downwind of their setts at sunset and stay very quiet. Maybe you will see them, maybe you won't, but there's a good chance. You've given yourself the best chance.

You want to put badgers off? Get close to their holes and shout 'Come out badgers, I want to see you! Come on. Now!'

You want to make sure you don't see a badger? Go shopping at Walmart or ASDA.

Queries about getting clear

I'm not sure what you mean by getting clear? How will I know if I've got there?

It's like any new territory- it's hard to get your bearings at first. Just keep noticing and learning, and after a while what was initially confusing starts to become more familiar. Subtle distinctions start to appear that you may not be able to make out at first. Can you recognise that you feel different in some ways from everyday life? Sometimes just sitting quietly will lead to noticeable differences. People often talk about feeling more peaceful. The rush and busyness of normal mental life subsides. Perhaps you become more aware of your body, of your breathing, of the sounds around that you normally miss.

I'm just not getting clear. Nothing happens.
Plenty is happening – just not necessarily what you are hoping for or expecting. Keep noticing what is happening. Welcome it, whatever it is. It's new. Get to know it.

You say it's like a spectrum – how will I know if I'm far enough along it?
Any distance along it from your everyday mind is far enough along to make a difference. The further you go the easier it is to shape up a poem from deeper within you. But write a poem from wherever you are at and see how you feel about it.

As you get more experienced then you will become familiar with a variety of different levels of clarity. Sometimes I like to ask myself 'What level of clarity am I in now?' Sometimes I use a scale of 1-10 to give me a rough idea (the upper reaches being places I haven't yet been to...). Remember that level of clarity is for the most part something we can influence but not control. What we can do is increase our skill levels so that with practice it is easier for us to enter and maintain certain levels of clarity.

How long does it take to reach a place of clarity?
Sometimes you can drop into a very clear space almost immediately. Sometimes you can sit for an hour before finally recognising that the everyday chatter has subsided. Sometimes after ten minutes you feel a level

of clarity, and then after fifteen minutes you realise you've lost it and have to start again. Sometimes, to be honest, it just doesn't happen. You get up at the end of your session and say to yourself, 'Well today my practice was just about concentrating on coming back to my breathing.'

Can you use other methods to get clear?

Meditation is not the only method you can use to access states that are clearer and deeper than everyday life.

Dancing, therapy, prayer, and others can also work.

We'll look at some of these in a little more detail in Section 4. For the time being we'll concentrate on sitting meditation (both classic and active) as the method of choice, because I think it has the most advantages of all the methods in terms of writing poetry, and because that's what this book is about.

Step 4 Allowing a topic to emerge

Let's assume you've been sitting for a while and you've noticed a greater sense of clarity than you are used to. From within this space you can now range over what you've noticed during this period, or what's happened recently in your life, and from that range allow one topic to emerge that you can focus on. Often this just happens: it's clear to you what that topic is. Sometimes, if it doesn't emerge, then you will need to choose a little more actively.

'Choosing' in this context has a particular shade of meaning. If we're not careful, then the action of choosing will start to activate our rational mind. We find ourselves looking for reasons to choose one topic before another; we start to consider the choices in a rational or semi-rational way. Ideally we are trying to avoid this as our rational minds, wonderful though they are in their own way, will interfere with our access to our deeper, creative parts. (We look at this tension in more detail later.)

Instead, 'choose' in as lightly an active way as you can. Some other ways to describe this process:

- pick something intuitively
- let something nudge into you and say yes to it
- be aware of what has the most energy and feeling for you and go with that
- feel your way into something that's right for this moment

When I use the word 'choose' in these next few examples, remember I'm meaning it in a light, intuitive way.

Maybe you've been noticing just your breathing. You could therefore choose your breathing as a topic. If you follow a meditation practice that emphasises breathing awareness, you can get quite involved in the nuances of breathing and really appreciate what it's like, and what it connects with. Breathing is more interesting than you might imagine. You may find that breathing features in your poems.

Maybe you've been aware of a walk you did yesterday, or the birdsong around you, or the leg that is aching more than usual. Choose one of those!

Maybe you have got caught up in a childhood memory, or a quotation from the Bible, or something a friend said to you last night. Choose one of those!

Maybe you had a fleeting awareness of peace beyond any which you have experienced before, or the tiniest tic on your upper lip, or the single sound of a bell in your mind. Choose one of those!

You get the picture? There is nothing - nothing! – that you cannot choose, and focus on, and write a poem about.. This whole universe is available for you to play in, and explore, and be creative around.

You've never thought of writing a poem about … before? Great! Go on and do it! Push your boundaries. You've never come across a poem about … before? Great! Go on and do it. Be the first. Push the boundaries for all of us.

Queries about allowing a topic to emerge
I can't seem to get a list at all.

Sometimes our mind does a blank. Just relax, breathe, and wait. Go back a step, and focus on just sitting and waiting for clarity and then noticing what happens. If there are still no possibilities, then 'no topic' may be your topic…

I can't make my mind up. Does it matter?

Not really. You can write a poem on anything, so why not do so? Choose one at random, or better, let it choose you. Imagine all the topics in a line before you. Which one edges out of the line and comes forward? Pick that one. Or ignore that pushy bad boy and pick the shy one at the back that's always being overlooked.

There's one I really don't want to look at but I can't get past it.

That's the one! But be realistic with yourself about timing here. If you're new to all this then don't start looking at the greatest trauma in your life right away. Yes, you probably need to look at it sometime, but not now. Wait till you are ready, and feeling confident enough to handle it.

If you're reluctant to look at something like, for example, an image of a butterfly because you find their fluttery wings irritating then that's more like it. There is always a rich source of energy and potential insight in material you're reluctant to look at.

When you are more experienced I recommend deliberately focusing on topics you don't want to focus on.

Step 5 Meditating around the topic

Take that topic and treat it as your object of meditation. This means that you hold it in your mind. In the same way that you might focus on your breathing, or a mantra, you focus on your topic. You notice what comes up for you around it. If you drift 'off' you simply return good naturedly to your topic.

What might come up around it? Every 'topic' will be different, and lead in different directions. But the principle is that anything may come up, and your 'job' is to notice what does arise, whatever it is. If you do this, then what comes may give you a sense of freshness, a new perspective on something you thought you already knew about, or an unexpected connection between two separate aspects of the topic.

Beyond a general sense of 'freshness', you may get an 'aha', a breakthrough insight that comes with a rush of excitement and recognition. A moment that says, 'Ah, so that's what it's about'. That's a great moment. That may well be your poem right there. You can enjoy the moment. You can also, if you wish, go back to the topic and see what else arises. Keep your mind open, and alert to the possibility of new insights developing.

We might visualise this process as a three-dimensional version of a 'mind-map' on a piece of paper. On the piece of paper your topic is written down in the bubble in the middle. Lines lead out from the central bubble. They are the connections to all the related thoughts, which you note down in bubbles round the edge of the paper.

In the three dimensional version in your mind, your central topic has little lines leading in all directions to your related images or thoughts. Sometimes you go from one related thought to another, and then another, and then realise you've got 'disconnected' from your topic, and need to go back.

The actual process in your mind will usually be much more messy and confused than the piece of paper version. The paper version is the neat, ordered version that comes afterwards.

An example

Let's see how this works in practice. Let's take 'baking bread' as our topic. Let's both spend a few minutes right now contemplating that subject and then compare notes. So sit now for a while with baking bread as your topic. What happens for you?

Back in a couple of minutes...

... how did you get on? Here's what happened for me. I had an image of one of those round brown loaves with a small round top-knot. It made me think 'France'. Then I saw very vividly the loaf tins, blackened and with a particular smell, that we used for baking bread at a community I once lived in. Then I realised that for a short while I'd been thinking about writing this book and had lost baking bread completely... so back to bread.

I got an image of a new baked loaf fresh out of the tin. Saw myself tearing a hunk off and ravenously eating the delicious hot, tasty, bread; yumm; started to move into other desires of the flesh - and stopped myself; realised that I was still with my body (not bread) and aware of my aching shoulders...

Was your process (if not the actual images) something like that? I suspect that it was similar. That's a pretty common pattern for me certainly. I start with the topic, I stay with the topic, I lose the topic, I go back to the topic, I lose the topic, I go back...

34

In other words, it's rarely simple, clear, and straightforward. It's more often messy, jumpy, and a bit confusing. But that is the territory that we often work in when we enter our inner world in this kind of way.

Sometimes it is different from this. Sometimes when I am in a state of unusual clarity, then it is as though I'm moving around amongst my thoughts in a spacious slow environment. I see them from all angles, and I see the connections between them. That's a special feeling. I hope you too can access it sometime.

Rule change

In this whole poetry-writing process up to now, what we've mostly been doing is following the 'classic' meditation guidelines. We've been sitting, following our breathing, calming our busy everyday mind, and entering, hopefully, a clearer state. In that clearer state we notice whatever arises, notice whatever arises hanging about for a while, and notice when it passes on. That's all. We aim to avoid engagement, getting lost in stuff, participating. We're witnesses.

For poetry writing, that witnessing may be sufficient. We may simply see whatever comes up, and simply write it up. Perfectly fine. Wonderful even.

But our aim here is to shape up poems from our deeper places, not develop a meditation practice. It's a crucial difference. In our poetry-writing world we have another option at this point.

We can choose to actively engage in our inner processes.

In a moment we'll look at the kinds of things you can do to 'actively engage'. If you have no existing meditation practice this will probably evoke some curiosity and interest in you.

If you have an existing meditation practice then it may evoke that curiosity, but also, to one degree or another, a sense of unease. He's asking me to break 'the rules'. The rules say no engagement and he wants me to engage. The rules say just witness and he wants me to stick my oar in. Ooh, I don't like this. What's going on?

Don't worry. I'm with you there. I still feel like that too. Bear with me if you can. I am not asking you to break the rules, so much as adopt a different set of rules for a particular situation. A poetry-writing situation. It will ease the transition if you do it with awareness. It's making a conscious choice to move away from classic meditation mode and into a related but different mode. We're not trying to sneak some shifts of emphasis in here by the back door. These two methods of inner work (developing a witness, and actively engaging) are related, but it is a really big deal to move from one to the other.

If you have difficulty with it, then bear witness to the difficulty, and the particular flavour it comes in.

Active engagement

So, when do we actively engage, and when do we stick with the classic approach?

As I mentioned above, sometimes the 'classic' witnessing approach is all we need.

At the other end of the spectrum of choice, so to speak, a very difficult issue sometimes comes up for us, and it feels really necessary to take active steps to work with it. Just witnessing it isn't effective. If we do that we may end up feeling very stuck.

Somewhere in the middle is a whole range of options. Remember, we're interested in generating poems, not in developing our capacity for staying in classic meditation mode, so we're free to try whatever we like and see what works.

We might decide that we'll only do active engagement when something comes up that disturbs us, makes us uncomfortable.

We might decide that we have no idea how to handle it, so we'll just do what feels right in the moment.

We may decide we love the idea of being free to choose and with no rules to follow.

We might decide that for a month we'll actively engage with every topic. What would that be like? What happens then?

If we have an existing meditation practice we might decide that we'll distinguish very carefully between meditating for poetry and meditating for meditation's sake: we'll do the different methods at different times, in different places, and not mix them up. That way, when we sit for poetry's sake, we may feel freer to actively engage in whatever way feels right.

So, why might we actively engage?

Because we can! Because there are now these tools available to us that enable us to engage in a useful, helpful, effective way. Because it stirs things up, and therefore, if we do it skilfully, it reveals more truth more quickly. Because it's a fascinating and interesting process to follow. Because it helps when we're confused, and a bit stuck, or very stuck. Because it enables us to write poems from deeper places - poems that we may not otherwise be able to write.

Because we are at heart curious, curious people, and we want to find out more ...

How do we actively engage with our inner processes?

Here are the basic suggestions to get you going. After that it's up to you. Invent your own ways. Adapt other people's. Meditate on the subject of 'ways of working on my inner processes' and see what comes up.

Amplify

If you have a visual image in your mind, what happens if you make it bigger? If you make it brighter? If you extend its reach?

If you have a sound in your mind, what happens if you make it louder? If you make it deeper in tone? Or more strident? Or if you surround it with a brass band accompanying it?

If you see yourself dancing, what happens if you give yourself permission to really dance, to dance exquisitely, wildly, or ecstatically?

One of the reasons for trying amplification is this. When things arise in our minds, then sometimes, because they're new, or we're uncertain about them, then the essential message or information or meaning contained within them may be very 'weak' or confused, and we just don't get that message. It's like a thin weak signal on the radio, maybe with lots of static around too. So, if that is the case, what do we do if we want to hear? We turn up the volume, and listen more carefully. With close attention, we start to pick up more easily on what we're hearing. We begin to decipher something that was unknown to us before.

I sat on a crowded train once. Further up the carriage a little girl sitting next to her father started to sing to herself. She did it completely unselfconsciously, while she was drawing and colouring. I found it very touching in and of itself. But as I sat there I found myself 'amplifying' the experience. I found myself seeing other trains travelling at the same time, some also with little girls sitting on them singing to themselves so very beautifully. Then as I amplified more, I saw that over the whole earth at this very moment were hundreds of little girls singing to themselves in contentment and happiness. I saw the lines that joined them all together. At that moment these connections were the most important lines on earth. More important than any other. It was a profound moment for me and one that I had to try to translate into a poem.

Dialogue

If an internal conversation opens up in your mind, keep it going, and see where it leads. Listen carefully! Ask questions and see what answers come up. Encourage all sides, especially if you are a little resistant to one side or the other, or one of the characters is not sympathetic to you. What about bringing in a different voice, or an additional person to the debate?

Keep a particular look out for those things that surprise you, or that you would not usually allow yourself to say, or hear. In your inner world, the normal 'rules' of polite society (whatever version you ascribe to...) do not apply. Characters can shout, or swear, or be rude, or sexual, or direct, or affectionate, or wildly happy, in ways that often aren't allowed. Here they are allowed. What happens? What do you notice?

In a way, this is a variation on the amplification tool. A dialogue exists – amplify it.

On another track, if a dialogue does not exist, consider starting one. Perhaps you are remembering a difficult incident from a few days before. It is in your mind, and you have decided to focus on it as your topic.

For example, at work someone, whom you like, ignored you for the whole day. You have been holding it in your mind, and you see and feel the whole day in a lot of detail, but no sense comes out of it, only a feeling of hurt. Start a conversation in your mind with the person. See where it leads and what emerges from it. If necessary bring in some others of your work colleagues. Do not assume that they will all say what they would say if you asked them 'in real life'. Listen for what they say in your mind. Look out for some heightened energy or interest (positive or negative) that indicates you are learning something new that may be relevant to your situation. Don't accept it as 'the truth' at once, but allow it as a possibility. Play with it some more. Allow it to be there.

Try it now. Close your eyes for a few minutes and consider a difficult situation you have recently encountered. Start a dialogue about it with the other people involved. See what comes up for you...

If we can support different strands of thought in these situations, different voices within us and in the world, then we start to tease out and loosen what may otherwise become a compacted block of feelings and thoughts that can end up quite quickly as rigid. It will then become fixed into the habitual way we interpret our life. In loosening the situation through a dialogue with different voices we are more likely to see things afresh and anew. That freshness will be insightful for us and may well be something we would like to shape into a poem.

Change perspective

Suppose you are looking at a particular event. You have a sense of it, but you feel there is more. Consider changing the perspective. From where are you looking at it now? You are looking at it from above? Get in amongst it instead. You are looking at it as an outsider? Become an insider.

You are close to the action? Take yourself away from the action. Slowly move up, up, and away. Or zoom to three miles distant. What happens then? What sort of difference does that make?

Perhaps you are remembering looking at a new butterfly emerging from its chrysalis. Become another butterfly perched alongside watching. Become the new creature itself. Become an angel of God watching the miracle of life transforming yet another creature into something new.

Resist!

Say 'no' and see what happens. Resist what is happening, and notice what happens then.

This is a powerful tool for uncovering significance. It's like putting your hand into a clear flow of water and watching the turbulence that results. What was transparent before becomes more visible. You see more of the flow, and the nature of the flow.

You are not trying to stop the flow, or suppress the flow, or move away from the flow. You are trying to learn more about the flow.

Here's an example that's just come to mind. I live near the Lake District in England. In spring-time the daffodils come into flower. Now I don't know about you, but it's very hard for me to see daffodils in the Lake District without thinking of Wordsworth and his famous lines (which I won't repeat here). What happens if I resist that energy, that tendency?

What happens is that I become aware of the powerful flow of cultural habit that takes me down the line of his words. They are great words, and he's a great guy, but I can't get to my own experience of the daffodils. I'm blocked off from that. The current of those words is too strong.

If I continue to resist this flow, however, a picture of Wordsworth himself pops into my mind. He's saying, 'I never intended those words to become a barrier. I just wrote a poem about a beautiful day. Please go past that and find your own experience and expression. That's what I did!'

Now I understand more about the situation, and what's happening to me, both as an individual, and as someone who does not exist apart from the cultural flow around him. That's an insight that could be shaped into a poem.

Hang out at the edge

This is about recognising that you are feeling uncomfortable about something, and deciding to stay there as long as you can and see what you notice. We could describe it as a special form of 'resist!' You are resisting your normal tendency to move away from discomfort. You're interested instead in learning about the discomfort and what is contained in that for you.

Other metaphors for this are 'lean a little closer to the fire' or 'stand at the doorway that leads into a new space, observing what is going on.'

In all these cases we're talking about recognising the discomfort, and then neither leaving it, nor rushing into it, but waiting, and watching, and learning. Later on you may decide to make your move, one way or the other.

Perhaps you are contemplating an experience of doing walking meditation on a retreat. Everyone is walking outside and the day is sunny. It's good. Suddenly you catch a little feeling of embarrassment. You notice it just as you try to move to a different memory. You decide instead to hang out with that. The embarrassment is a strong sensation in your body, and you want to leave it, but what happens if you stay there instead, just being with it, at the edge of what you can manage? Who knows what will come out of that!

Queries on meditating around the topic

I seem to be 'off' much more than I'm 'on'. What to do?

It happens all the time. You're with the rest of us here. Just keep coming back. Enjoy the return – that can be a great feeling. Usually it's just a question of developing your skill at this over time. To help yourself, make sure you choose a topic with plenty of juice in it for you. Usually the more energy and feeling, the easier it is to stay with it.

Sometimes when I go 'off topic' I get really interested in the new topic.

That's a really interesting dilemma! I'd say there are two answers here. If you're just starting off, then the sensible advice is to keep practising with your original intention – that's the skill you're trying to develop which will stand you in good stead in the years to come as you contemplate something which may transform into a satisfying poem. Otherwise the risk is that you will just lose yourself moving on from one interesting topic to the next and then the next and then... Remember, you could always come back to that interesting new topic in a different session.

However if you are reasonably confident in your capacity to hold to a topic then it is an interesting experiment to see if you can shift to a different topic. The risk is you may lose track of what you have discovered around the first one. But if, in order to mitigate this risk, you pause briefly, say, to note down insights from the first area, then you are out of 'the space' and may not be able to get back in. I tend to trust to my capacity to retain in my mind the gist of what's important and not risk breaking the spell, so to speak. Of course one of the interesting questions may well be: what is the connection for you between topic one and topic two? Maybe there is an insight, a truth, to emerge between the two, if you can move back and forward between them.

I keep focusing on the topic but it all seems very ordinary – I haven't had a sense of freshness or insight.

Keep going anyway. This may be your judging mind rushing to judgement! Maybe you haven't yet learned to recognise what is fresh and new – sometimes the signs are quite subtle and take time to get to know.

Maybe the 'ordinary' is what you need to focus on, as a topic. What does it feel like? Look like? What do you associate with it? Where does it lead to if you keep coming back to it again and again? What happens if you welcome the sense of 'ordinary' and really appreciate it?

This may also be one of the barriers (critical voice: 'I'm no good at this') that we look at in more detail in Section 3 of this book.

Will 'breaking the rules' harm my existing meditation practice?

It will influence it for sure. Partly because everything influences everything else – we can't keep our existing meditation practice pure and separate from anything. It doesn't work like that.

Your safeguard is awareness – you are deliberately entering into a different mode of inner work. That means you can also choose not to enter that different mode, or to enter, and then exit.

In that sense you may experience a greater freedom within, and appreciation for, your existing practice. There is a related but different way of doing things; you've tried it, and confirmed that for 'ordinary' meditation purposes, you prefer your existing practice.

You may experience a boost to your meditation practice. Maybe you'd got a little stale, got lost in the form, were going through the motions. It happens.

So 'breaking the rules' may be a distracting deviation from your existing meditation practice, it may be a support for it, or it may become your practice. Beware! Or, be aware!

Are there more resources for looking further at active engagement?

I'll mention one book in this area that's been important for me. It came before I got interested in 'classical' meditation, and therefore before I developed my ability and skill in that area.

The book is 'Working on Yourself Alone' by Arnie Mindell. He takes his broadly psychotherapeutic approach (he calls it 'process work' or 'process oriented psychotherapy') and applies it to the area of inner contemplation. So when 'disturbances' come up in your mind, which in standard meditation you would ignore, he actively takes them up, and works with them. In his book, there are lots of examples of how to do this, and what happens. I've found it fascinating and valuable. If you're interested in taking this kind of study further, this book (which is quite technical) is a great resource.

But it's not necessary to read it in order to write poems.

A short pause while we consider a more general point

We're about to move into the verbal stage, so at this point we should note that the process up to this point has been general, but now it becomes particular. We're interested in shaping up a poem, so that's what we're going to focus on. But it doesn't have to be that way.

We've been looking deeply at what we're calling a topic. It may be an object, or an action, or an event, or feeling, or experience, or conflict, for example. Our plan is to take whatever aspects of the truth of that topic that we've uncovered and translate them into a poem. That's what we're setting out to do.

We could equally work to translate them into a song. Or an essay. Or a piece of music. A tapestry. An action in the world. A note in our journal. An email to a friend.

It doesn't have to be verbal. Some of the possibilities I've mentioned above are non-verbal. But for the purposes of this book, we're going verbal. We're bringing words into play.

We're going with poem: words, concepts, phrases, arrangement of words on the page. That's our choice today.

Step 6 Allowing words to arise

When the vision, or experience, or topic or event in your mind has been around for a while and you have developed a feel for it, start to allow words to appear around it, and notice what they are. Let words, and phrases, appear, and let them build up and lead to other words and phrases.

Notice that this is a very light, effortless, invitational process. We allow it to happen. We trust the process, we trust the infinite playful creativity of our minds and the infinitely playful universe of which they are a part.

We're not cudgeling our brains to find the 'right' word or phrase, the 'right' metaphor.

We're noticing the words that appear, but at this early stage we don't hold on to them, we don't try to grab them and fix them. This is because they might not be the final words for today. They might just be the opening into our verbal self, the doorway into the richer verbal storehouse beyond. So we just watch, and notice, and notice our responses too. Maybe there's some word or phrase that moves us and makes us smile, or sigh a little. That sounds promising...

Words can easily lead to other words, but we're not looking for a verbal game of consequences, we're looking for words that express the truth of our insights and experience. So we can also keep going back to the non-verbal image or topic that we started with. We can check our verbal manifestations against the original experience. How does it match up? Do we feel happy enough?

Maybe there are some really attractive words but they are not truthful enough. Sadly we have to let them go. Maybe there are some less attractive words but they do a great job. We hold them there, lightly, and come back to them if needed.

If a particular pattern starts to feel right, then we can stick with that and let it grow.

We're shading here into the next stage of shaping a form for your poem. This transition isn't necessarily clear and stark. It might be, but equally it might be a seamless, undetectable shift through into the next stage. We'll pause here anyway, and consider some further questions about this stage.

Some queries about allowing words to arise
Nothing useful comes, only verbiage.

If we rush to judgement (and we all do it at times) and decide that something is not useful, no good, a waste of time, then that judgement will ensure that the judgement is true. It will be no good.

It's like seeing a seedling oak tree in the ground, pulling it out and looking hard at it and saying, 'Well, that's not a real tree,' and tossing it aside. It isn't a real tree yet, and now it never will be.

For this or any creative process to work, we have to suspend our judgement, our critical faculties. We have to create a safe and protected growing space in which something new and unknown will grow. It's not wholly in our control as to what grows. It is in our control to protect the space, or destroy the space.

There is nothing wrong, as such, with our judgement. Judgement is a crucial and important part of our way of being in the world.

Let's really appreciate and applaud our judgement: 'Hail judgement!'

But let's keep judgement firmly in its rightful place. And that's not here.

My rational organising mind wants to make up a poem straight away.

Yes, so does mine sometimes. Old habits die hard. Particularly if you've been used to writing poems in a different way, you may well want to get on with it and work to get the finished article. That's what you do when you write a poem isn't it? You write it!

For the time being, just notice the impatience and go back to your topic. Keep faith with that and with the creativity of your deeper being. Give it a chance. See what happens.

Can words come too soon?

Yes they can and do. There isn't necessarily a clear distinction between this phase (allowing words to arise) and the previous one (focusing on a topic). Sometimes there is a clear boundary: we recognise we have focused enough, and we decide to allow words to come on the scene, and here they come. Fine.

Sometimes, often even, words start arriving of their own volition. We're verbal people, we live in a verbal world. Words are used to having their own way. They assume they are part of the family and can turn up anytime they like. And they do.

Sometimes that also is fine: we're more or less ready for them, so let's go with it and see what happens as we move into the 'words arising' stage.

But sometimes it is too soon. We're not ready. We need more time with our topic to get a sense of it. We're pretty clear on this, so when we notice words starting to arise, we simply return to our topic. We ignore the words and they get the message and go away.

Sometimes it's not so clear. We're not sure. Sometimes words have sneaked back in without us really noticing, and here we are seeing and hearing phrases and concepts. How do we tell if this is happening? What do we do?

Look out for signs, possibly quite subtle, of feeling a little weary with the words. They don't quite have a freshness to them. They are not quite there. You've heard them before in some way. You may feel this in your body as a slight tiredness or lack of interest. Maybe a subtle sense of duty: 'Ah yes, time to move on I know.'

If that's the case, go back to your topic. The words have arrived too early at the party. They have to go off somewhere and wait till the time is right for them to come in. It'll be good for them. They can contemplate their position in your world and recognise they have no rights here. You can go back to the source: your inner being, your focus on the topic, and your relationship with that. There's a freshness there you can tap into, and, often, you'll recognise when it's now OK to let the words come.

I can't hold all the ideas that come up. I'm scared I'll forget something important.

I'm sorry to say this but you can't hold all the ideas that come up and you will forget many things that are important. That's the way it is here. And there will be feelings of panic, or grief, or irritation that go with that.

'I had an amazing insight, a truth that would have changed the whole world, and then I got caught up in planning my next shopping trip to Sainsbury's and by the time I realised what had happened, the insight had gone and I can't get it back!'

Ever heard the famous story of Coleridge writing 'Kubla Khan'? My wife Mary and I recently walked past the farmhouse in Somerset where it happened. There's a blue plaque on the wall: 'This is where Coleridge was in the middle of writing Kubla Khan, which had come to him in a great vision, when he was interrupted by a man from Porlock knocking at the door, and by the time he got back to writing, he'd forgotten the rest of the vision.'

No, only kidding – about the plaque anyway. The story is true. (By the way, surely there really should be a plaque?)

We felt for him, because we've most of us been there.

It's just what happens sometimes, and the main compensation is that the universe is vast, and creativity is infinite, and therefore all sorts of other truly amazing insights and deeply satisfying poems are just around the next bend, or just after the next moment.

Step 7 Shaping a form

This is an interesting and often tricky part. You are moving from a partially shaped cloud of words and phrases that are merged with your experience, to a concrete particular sequence of words that can only point to parts of your experience. There are choices to make and it's sometimes painful.

This stage is so crucial, and so interesting, and therefore so long, that I've had to break it down into a lot of smaller sections. So, just to let you know, we'll be considering:

- a part for the rational mind, plus a warning
- how the process actually works
- how you can support the process and what to avoid
- what is form and shape, and who decides what's right?
- how form is important to communication
- is there a trade-off between making it easier for the reader and being truthful?
- what you can do if you're not sure about the right form
- another aspect of form
- the painfulness of choosing form
- why poetic form can help powerful communication
- an example in detail
- queries on 'shaping a form'

A part for the rational mind, plus a warning

This is a point where your rational mind, the conceptual, does start to play a small part. The skill is in allowing it to play its appropriate part at the appropriate time, and to prevent it from taking over completely, which it will usually do at the drop of a hat if you let it.

The reason not to allow this is that we are still in the special creative space where unusual, unexpected things may need to happen. We need to protect that space as long as is right. For most of us, that is longer than we're used to, and longer than our rational mind will like.

So how might this stage actually work?

Let's assume you've got to a place where there is a cloud of words and phrases around your topic. There is some sense of what the poem might be. There is a vague shape to it.

Your first move is to go through it in your mind from whatever feels like the beginning, to whatever feels like the end. Then do it again, and again, and again. Some parts you will repeat each time, but some will change - and that's the point. The poem is refining itself in your mind. It is moving further along the route from non-conceptual to conceptual, and you are observing and recording that process. It may feel that this is happening without your conscious input, and if that is the case, you can enjoy this privileged state.

When you go over your sequence of words in your mind time after time then it starts to come together as a whole. The parts all influence each other.

Sometimes this is a very simple, straightforward process.

And sometimes it's more confused and less straightforward.

And sometimes it feels very confusing indeed.

Here's some of what can happen:

It may turn out that when you get to the end, there's a way in which the beginning needs to change to take account of the end.

It may be that the order you started with becomes changed around, with the beginning going to the middle, and the middle to the end.

It may be that just when you feel you've got a form emerging something new crops up and just has to be included.

It may be that what you thought was the main theme or message at the start of the process, drops off in influence, or drops out altogether.

It's altogether likely that at times you find yourself somewhere else entirely and have to delicately but firmly take yourself back to where you had been focusing.

It may be that you feel uncomfortable with a process that you are not really in control of. The answer to this discomfort is that you are going to have to tolerate uncertainty and mystery for a period, at exactly the same time as part of you is desiring a fixed and complete result (and desiring it now!).

How to support this process and what to avoid

While the poem is gradually (or quickly) adopting its shape within you, you can help the process in three ways:

1.   stay out of it as much as possible and just let it happen

2.   intervene in the process from a feeling perspective. You notice when you feel that something is right and true. Some phrase or some shape brings a smile to your being and you just know this is it, or nearly it. You know that you are on the right lines...

3. intervene from a thinking perspective. You start to try to work out what could fit here, or be expressed there. You start to work on it. You start to worry at it.

I think you can probably guess by now that if you want to shape up a satisfying poem from deep in your being, I recommend you focus your efforts on 1 and 2, and leave method 3 for some future time when you're more experienced and can approach it in a suitably experimental mood.

What is form and who decides what's right?

It often happens that the right 'form' emerges from this process of repeatedly going through your poem in your mind. Often but not always. We'll deal with what to do if it doesn't in a minute.

By 'form' I mean the shape of the poem as a whole, and therefore also to some extent the shape of the poem on the page when you come to write it down. Form and shape will also encompass such things as the perspective it's written from, whether there is repetition, including perhaps a chorus, whether it's a story, or variations on a theme, or a prayer. We'll look at these shortly.

How do we know what is the 'right' form? Is it a technical issue?

It's more a case of asking ourselves a different kind of question:

What form would fit with the meaning? What form best reflects and amplifies what I'm expressing?

Another way of asking this is: What form would please me here, what would feel right?

This is not the same as asking, what shape would look good on the page? What form do other people mostly use? What form would say to people I'm a cool and clever poet, with special gifts? ("I have special powers. Do not try these things for yourselves at home!")

You can experiment with form. It's your poem, it's your form. The basic point about form, in the context of this book, is that the 'right' form is the one that best helps convey the truths and insights you are seeking to express and communicate. Nothing else counts. Nothing.

Not what anybody else says. Not what your internal critic says. Not what your local creative writing tutor says. Not what most other poems use. Not what Wordsworth, or Keats, or John Donne uses. Not even what Rumi (in translation or the original) uses.

Got that? Good!

How form is important to communication

Form or shape is also important, probably more important, for the second of our criteria on what makes an effective poem from deep. We're looking for truthfulness to our experience, and we're looking for effective communication of that experience to someone else (assuming that's the route we're probably going down).

Because we have had the experience ourselves, we don't necessarily need much to remind us of what it was actually like, especially if it was powerful, and especially if it was recent. I only have to say 'my first look inside Durham Cathedral' to myself and I'm back with the overwhelming feelings, mysteries and sights of the first hour I spent there earlier this year. It's like a little shorthand note to myself that jogs my memory and takes me straight there.

But that's not much use if I want to share that experience with someone else. I can say 'my first look inside Durham Cathedral' to someone and they may never have been there, so it means little to them. Or if they have been there, they will have had their own experience, possibly similar to mine, or possibly very different from mine.

If I am able to write about that experience in a detailed, truthful way, then I should be able to communicate some of the subtleties, insights and meaning of what occurred at the time, and about which I reflected afterwards. I hope for two things here: that I will remind myself of the details and intrinsic power of that experience (because even powerful memories can fade and lose their definition) so that I am supported on my path of exploration and inspiration, and, two, that this may be inspiring to someone else, and encourage them to connect more deeply in their own way with Durham Cathedral, or any other aspect of our universe.

Is there a trade-off between making it easier for the reader and being truthful?

The shape or form of the poem has an impact on how accessible your insights and experiences are to someone else.

As a poet we have some choices here. And sometimes we have some difficult choices: how far am I willing to go towards easing the way for the potential reader if that means I lose some of my truthfulness? As poets we live with that tension most of the time, but sometimes it's more apparent than at other times.

It's not necessarily within our total control as to how clear or opaque our poems end up. If we are shaping poems in a context where we trust an inner creative process, then sometimes the process just comes up with a difficult form and phrasing. In that case we are asking our readers to struggle with the language and shape because that seems to be required.

This is a different case from where, say, a writer seems to deliberately choose obscure language and difficult phrasing in order, apparently, to be obscure and difficult. Hmmm.

And then there is the question of the receptivity of the reader. If someone, for example, doesn't really 'get' in the slightest way what my subject is, (God, Buddha nature, weakness, amoeba...) then my poem on that subject could be as clear as you like to some people but will likely remain meaningless to them.

It's better to be clear with yourself about how accessible you would like your poems to be. Remember the intention? We can incorporate in our intention, either overtly or implicitly, our wish for our poems to be as clear as possible to other people.

Or vice versa. There's nothing wrong, per se, with obscure, convoluted, or difficult poems. You could simply say 'I like my poems to be hard to read, impossible to understand, or so vague as to mean almost anything.' (I'm trying to be fair here but you can probably tell I'm failing.) And you could go on and say 'and if you can't understand them, then that's your loss.'

I've always thought it's pretty easy to make simple stuff out to be really complicated. It's much harder to make complicated stuff simple to understand (without losing the depth). I'm not interested in the first, and I am interested in the second. Making complicated stuff a bit easier to grasp is my intention in this book.

Whatever you decide you prefer, my recommendation as ever, is to do it with awareness and consciousness.

Not sure about the right form?

If a form emerges at the same time as the right words emerge, and you're reasonably happy with it, then it's probably the right form. The poem can continue to emerge as a whole, and you're set for the next stage: writing down.

Sometimes I'm surprised by how quickly and simply a poem can emerge. I still, even after years of experience that contradicts this, somehow expect a poem to be difficult, hard to write, complex and sophisticated. I still somehow assume it's not worth anything much unless it's formed from hours of sweat and blood. Not so, my friends, not necessarily so.

Sure, some poems come with birthing pains and hard labour. But others slip out easily and well, and are beautiful in themselves from that moment. In effect the hard work has not been missed out – but it's been done in the years of living and practice and effort that led up to the emergence of the poem. One of the skills you are developing as a poet therefore is to recognise when a truthful poem has simply and easily emerged, and to leave it at that without any more interference.

However, what if the right form doesn't emerge?

The failure of the right form to emerge will feel something like this: you have images, or feelings, and snatches of words, or whole phrases, and a sense of something wanting to come into being, but you don't sense how they all fit together, you don't sense what the connections are. It's like a morass, or a thicket of thorns, or a disjointed collection of bits and pieces in a jumble sale. You probably find yourself drifting off a lot. You may find yourself thinking 'ah well, no poem today'.

If the right form doesn't emerge then you can still skilfully help the process. You don't need to give up at this point.

The basic guidance comes, as usual, to this: be aware, be mindful.

A definition of mindfulness is: 'being aware of what is happening, while it's happening, whatever it is'. A shorter way of saying this might be 'conscious awareness.'

In the creative space where a poem is being shaped within you, then the more awareness you can bring to the party, then the easier you will find it. Mindfulness is neither a mystery nor an accident, but a skill that you can learn and develop over time.

Wherever you are now on the 'capacity for mindfulness' spectrum, you already have enough awareness to shape a poem. No need to delay!

If what is happening within you is confusing and difficult then your first move is to be aware of that and recognise that that is your current reality. Also notice if any feelings of frustration or disappointment come up – and if possible let them go by.

I'll take you through some examples of what I call implicit prompts, and some examples of explicit prompts to help you at this stage.

Implicit prompts

This is where you are noticing what is already happening with the poem, and simply amplify and develop that.

For example, amongst the confusion, maybe there is one particular phrase that comes up which makes you smile a little, is interesting for you, expresses a truth in a new way for you. You could take that as the core, and develop from there. Maybe that phrase opens the poem. Maybe it opens and closes it. Maybe it's a refrain, a chorus, running through it, around which other insights or descriptions can grow.

Or you can go back to the original core event or image and refresh yourself there, as at a fresh spring of water. This is where the impetus and energy for the poem comes from – this is where the poem starts, even though it may end up in a different or an unexpected place. But you can go back there and then flick back to the words you have, and go back, and keep doing that, and see whether some new emphasis or focus emerges that then clarifies the right form for you.

Or you may notice that one part of what you are holding, circulating among, or looking at, has more energy for you, more interest. You can let yourself focus in on that. In doing so, you may have to let go of some of the other stuff, though that may be painful.

Explicit prompts

This is a slightly tricky process because in the middle of what is still mainly a creative, imaginative, non-conceptual process, we are moving a little bit into the rational, conceptual, realm. The purpose is to help the imaginative side, but the risk is that because the rational side is so strong and habitual it will take over. So as lightly as we can, we might touch on these questions:

Person?

This is shorthand for 'is this poem going to be expressed from the first, second, or third person, or a combination?' In other words, will the poem come from an 'I' stance, or a 'you' or 'we' stance, or a 'he', 'she', 'it', 'they' stance. There are other possibilities. Just description, no person at all. Or something more universal: 'one', 'the one who...'

Sometimes just asking this question is enough to tip the form into the right place. You might realise that you'd assumed it was going to be a poem from your personal point of view, from 'I'. But actually that's too vulnerable a standpoint for you at the moment and the poem won't emerge. But shape it from the third person ('the traveller saw that...' 'he understood that...' 'a friend I know fell...') and maybe something comes together more easily.

We can also experiment with 'which person?' at a later stage, and we'll look at that under 'editing.'

Story?

Start from the beginning, go through the middle, get to the end. Tell a story, and we all know what the form is. We like stories. Humans have been telling them ever since they invented enough words to do so.

Length?

Sometimes I get stuck because I've assumed the poem has to be a certain, 'proper', poem-like length. So I may be able to move on when I realise that for this poem, four lines is just fine. If that's what the poem is, then that's what it is. Alternatively I may be able to move on when I realise I don't have to condense what I have into a page. Maybe this poem is just a really long poem, and that's how it is.

Dialogue?

Are you having a conversation in your head between different people (real or imagined), or between different parts of you?

Sometimes you can assume you have to get past the dialogue to the 'real' poem beyond. Sometimes the dialogue is the poem.

Focus in?

Maybe you are trying to pull too much material together under one heading. Maybe the connections aren't there and it's just too complicated. Focusing in on just one element of what you are holding in your mind may be the way through.

This may mean however, letting go of something that feels important or precious. And that, as we know, can be hard to do. Let go of something? Not me!

Resisting?

What can happen is that we get to an area which, for various reasons, is a bit too hot for us to handle at the moment, and a part of us therefore resists the emergence of a poem about it. This is an interesting topic and we'll look at it in more detail later in the book (Section 4: Moving on to a different level; 'What if the subject feels too big?'). However, sometimes, just asking the question at this point helps us realise that (a) yes we do have some resistance but that (b) having acknowledged it we can just move on.

Body, breathing?

What am I feeling in my body? What's happened to my breathing? Maybe I've got into stress because there's no form emerging! Maybe I can feel the tension in my belly or shoulders. If I relax here and breathe again, then something that has got stuck in me may start to shift again. Who knows what effect that will have on my poem?

New?

This is a reminder to yourself that there may already be a form here, but you are simply not recognising it. It may simply be unfamiliar to you. Or it may be completely new, never seen before in the universe. Thomas Hardy liked to experiment with form, and he manifested many different forms, even while working within the more formal rhyme and metre poetic tradition of a century and more ago.

With relatively free verse there's an infinite variety to create and choose from. Remember, the form is up to you.

Usual?

Perhaps you have some familiar forms that you habitually use. Here's a chance to remind yourself that you are not pursuing novelty for its own sake. You are looking for a form that will give effective expression to what is within you. That may well be a form that's worked well for you in the past. You will have, or develop, your own list.

Remember, just as there is no limit within the universe as to what you can write a poem about, there is no limit in the whole universe to what form you can use to express that subject. It's yours, only yours.

A great question to ask

Sometimes, when I seem to be stuck in confusion amongst many possible forms and many possible poems, I ask myself, 'If I had to write a poem now, what would it be?'

That question can be enough at times to tip me from endless potential into actual form. An answer comes up, usually with all kinds of doubts attached to it. But with a little focus it often then transforms into the poem I was always going to write.

The painfulness of choosing form

OK, so there you are, in a space of greater clarity than usual, and you are contemplating some topic that is important to you. You are perhaps enjoying the sense of connection with it all. You are seeing stuff you haven't seen before, the way things fit together. That sense of connectedness just seems to be able to go on and on without limit. This is fun! This is meaning! Meaning is flowing all through you and around you and this topic. Your thoughts and feelings are there and they are real to you. All is possible, all is available. There is no limit.

You can feel yourself wanting to move on and share this wonderful clarity and meaning in a poem.

And you try. But gradually you realise (again!) that you can't get it all in. That's impossible. A limitless sense of connection doesn't translate to a limited series of words on a page. That's just not how it works. You know that really. You've known that before. But that doesn't stop you from feeling, in one form or another, the pain of that.

Here's an analogy. When my children were little they would often be completely involved in their games. Perhaps an elaborate imaginative role play game involving one or other of their extensive collections of little plastic figures. I, the parent, might say something ordinary like 'Lunch is ready'. But in doing this I have interrupted where interruption is not welcome. A great cry of pain and frustration goes up: 'You've broken the game!'

You've broken the game.

I've broken the game.

When we try and move from the swirl of thought and feeling and image in our minds to words on a page we are effectively breaking the game. We are moving from one game to a different type of game. They are related, but not the same.

It would be like me saying to my children 'Hey, kids, time to move from playing with your thundercat figures, to writing about playing with your thundercat figures.' Hmm. You see the problem there?

Now sometimes that is just fine. We're ready to move on, we're satisfied with the game but it's finished. Later, after lunch, we will go and do a different game that involves writing all sorts of descriptions of thundercat figures and their amazing adventures.

Similarly, sometimes our transition from inner swirl to outer form of poem is just fine and dandy. All goes well and smoothly and we are getting on with it in a satisfying and joyful way. What can be more pleasing than emerging from a clear and insightful state with a form of words that satisfies us because it does justice to our experience? Really, can anything beat that?

And sometimes our transition from inner swirl isn't fine at all.

If we move into form we will lose so much! All those possibilities will disappear and be replaced by just one outcome. The game will be broken, and we won't get it back. Even if we get back to the game, it won't be the same game. That broken game will be gone for ever.

Even if we do go on and try, our efforts to translate all that wonderfulness into a poem will fail. The words will be inadequate to the task. It's hardly worth the effort of trying.

No wonder feelings of disappointment, frustration, pain and suffering arise in these circumstances. No wonder we don't want to move on. No wonder we cling to the inner swirl, and resist moving into the outer form. Who in their right minds heads towards suffering?

And one option is not to do so, not to break the intensity of the game, but to stay in it. We're not small children. No-one can make us have lunch when we don't want to. (Can they?) No-one is making us write a poem. (Are they?) We can ignore the poem. We can stay with the swirl, and the inner sense of satisfaction, and peace and connectedness.

Sometimes staying in the space is the right thing to do

Maybe you're in a great space and maybe it's important to stay there as long as you can. If you're not used to inner spaces of especial clarity and beauty, then there is actually a skill in getting to know them, and learning to tolerate them. This may sound strange – joy, pleasure? What's not to like? But we have a habitual tolerance around joy, love and peace. When we get stretched along those lines, we know it's good for us, and we enjoy it for a period, and then it gets too much. And out we come.

Another poem will always form itself at some point, but this particular space will never return in the same way. There's a case for being in it, being with it, and enjoying it, just as long as you can. It's your inner space, and it's therefore your choice.

In classical meditation terms, by the way, we also would not come out of the space – not in order to write a poem anyway, because that would not be part of our agenda.

We would stay in (while the session continued) and whatever came up – joy, connectedness, clarity, bliss even – we would be aware of, but not be attached to, not lost in, and not seeking to keep, or return to. In this practice we would develop our awareness, and eventually transcend our attachment to all states of mind, or attachment to any of our internal processes.

As I've said before, in this book we are not overtly concerned with learning about meditation for its own sake. There are plenty of resources out there for those who want to do that. But in entering a meditation-like space, and from there shaping up poems, we can certainly throw light on the meditation process in an interesting and useful way.

And sometimes the right thing to do is to move on

That's because the process has a life of its own. Remember our intention? Our intention is to shape up a poem. We can't always do what we want. The greater aim subsumes the moment to moment wishes and desires. In order to do what we intend we have to be a little disciplined, a little determined.

So we may be faced with a reluctance to go on because of the suffering that brings up, and yet we go on anyway, through the discomfort, because that is what we are required to do if we are to fulfil our current purpose.

It's helpful if we can recognise this pattern, and be aware of it. We can be practical about it. 'It's just what happens sometimes. Go on anyway'. We can be understanding, 'I know this is painful but in a short while it will all be over and there will be a really good poem and I'll feel fulfilled.' We can find whatever method works for us to go onwards, let go of our attachment to swirling potential form, and move forward into definite out-in-the-world form. While also feeling whatever aspect of discomfort comes up for us at this time.

Why is this sometimes so difficult?

Remember a few pages back I said this:

If we move into form we will lose so much! All those possibilities will disappear and be replaced by just one outcome. The game will be broken, and we won't get it back. Even if we get back to a game, it won't be the same game. That broken game will be gone for ever.

Even if we do go on and try, our efforts to translate all that wonderfulness into a poem will fail. The words will be inadequate to the task. It's hardly worth the effort of trying.

What I didn't say at the time is that these two points (we lose so much; no words can be adequate) are not only difficult for us, but they are also true. It is so.

When we move from the non-verbal to the verbal we lose not just a lot, we lose everything. The direct experience is gone, it's over. Everything is gone. It can't be reclaimed. That's impossible.

And of course the words are inadequate. This is not to diminish words themselves. Words are extraordinary. Our capacity to communicate with each other using words, and mutually comprehend each other, is miraculous. But words cannot reproduce the experience. It's impossible.

However, once we recognise these two impossibilities, then we know what is actually going on. We are with the reality that exists. That leaves us freer to experiment and enjoy ourselves. What we're actually doing is entering into a different experience. In the new experience we are attempting to point towards the first, to evoke a sense of it, and to communicate the meaning that has arisen around it for us.

When we are shaping a poem we are working (usually) on a previous experience of some kind to bring it into a readable form, but the shaping is also its own experience as it is happening. We can bring our awareness to the shaping as much as to our sense of the remembered experience.

And when people read the poem, then that is a new experience that is arising in that moment, for them.

Maps and territories

This pattern is an example of the map and territory distinction. If I write a book about visiting France, and you read it, you may experience it as an inspirational description, or perhaps as entertaining. You may experience the book, as, perhaps, accurate and learned. But it's not an experience of France. To experience France you have to get on a boat or train and go there. The book is like a map. It points the way, and helps you to access the place. But to experience the place you have to go there yourself.

You may have an inspirational experience of Buddha nature, a sense of direct connection with Reality. You may write that up in a deep poem. Your poem is still a map of the experience. It is not the experience. It may inspire people to move closer to that experience themselves, and may show them a way there, but they still have to do that themselves for themselves.

Spiritual tradition parallels

Spiritual traditions often talk about this area in a way that parallels what we have been discussing here in the context of shaping poems.

In most Buddhist traditions for example there is a distinction between the Relative (the everyday world) and the Absolute (ultimate Reality). Teachings given in the Relative world can point the way towards the Absolute, but they are not the Absolute. A person can only apprehend the Absolute through their own being in their own way.

The classic metaphor is to say that teachings are like a finger pointing at the moon. The finger shows the direction to go in in order to get there, but it is not the moon itself.

If we remember that our poems are like teachings, like a finger pointing at the moon, not the moon (the experience) itself, then our suffering around our inadequacy should be less.

Why poetry can be powerful

Let's go back to a place where you have been, say, sitting in clarity, and focused on a topic. You have been persistent, and disciplined, and fortunate, and today you feel blessed to have gained insight into some aspect of your life. You wish to mark that in some way, and bring it more overtly into your daily life. We have earlier in the book established that you could do that in a variety of ways: through some kind of art -dance, a song, a drawing – or simply through a different form of action in your life - inviting an old friend to a meal, starting a new project, fixing the broken tap.

We also established that at this point you can go verbal, and we focused on poetry, the main topic of this book. But why poetry? There are other verbal forms of expression.

You could, at one end of the spectrum, write a learned article in serious academic prose. And at the other end you could jot the words that come to you on a piece of paper, cut it up, scatter the pieces on the floor, take a photo and make it available to other people. Both those extremes, and everything in between, are valid choices. It's your insight, your inner life, and it's up to you how you express it.

So why poetry? - 1

Sometimes this will be an emotional choice. Poetry has resonance and energy for us. We like it. We want to be someone who writes poetry. We know that poetry is a form that people often turn to when they have something of emotional and personal importance to say.

As a child, I had a strong connection with my Aunt Mary, one of my mother's sisters. She was loving and gentle. She loved me and looked after me at times, and she wrote poetry. I identified with that capacity. I knew from my own experience that it could be done. Someone close to me was a serious, committed, poet.

Maybe you have your own version of this story. What is your emotional connection with poetry? How has it been in your life? Were you made to read it at school, and study it, and write about it so that it put you off? Or were you enthused and inspired? Was there a connection in some other context? Why not sit with this as a topic, see what emerges for you, and write a poem about it? You could call it 'My poetic CV'.

Sometimes, strangely, the poetry might choose us. I had dabbled in writing poetry at different periods of my life. In 2010, just after my partner of many years and I had got married, I found myself 'called' to take poetry writing seriously and pursue it in a disciplined way for a while. I needed to give it a proper chance to emerge and develop. I was reluctant! I didn't want to do it! Poetry was not me, not at this time. Could I even do it? What if I couldn't?

I started, and continued, in secret for quite a while. I didn't choose poetry, poetry chose me, and I've been involved in this relationship ever since.

So there might be some element of this story in your life too. If we enter into a space of clarity and connect more deeply with our inner life, then the unknown emerges in us, and can lead us in unexpected directions. Where might your unknown take you? You could sit with that for a while as a topic, and see what emerges...

So why poetry? - 2

Poetic form provides a recognised and familiar structure that is yet flexible enough to reflect a myriad different meanings, experiences and perspectives. Prose can do a lot, but it's usually geared towards a linear rational exposition: A to C via B. With complete sentences and other recognised structures. There's a lot of scope for variation but a lot of formal restrictions.

With poetry you are not restricted in these ways. So your experience has not been linear but more a meditation on a theme? Fine, you can repeat a phrase throughout and run different responses off it. Your experience has been an emotional roller coaster which you don't really yet understand? Fine, you can just put out a variety of different emotional colours without having to tie them together in a way that makes rational sense.

Yes, all of these things can be done in prose (or random, cut-up words) but the form remains the one form: prose. With a variety of poetic form available you have a big opportunity to reflect your meaning in the form as well as the words.

So why poetry? - 3

You've got to 'get' stuff yourself – life, insight, meaning, experience. For example, you know you've got to 'get' love yourself: practise love, feel love, experience love. Reading about love, talking about love, thinking about love, understanding love: none of these is the same as 'getting' love. They might prepare the ground, they might point the way, they might help you to stick with it, and tolerate it, and enjoy it when you experience it. But you have to 'get' love yourself.

A poem can support this process. When you focus on something within you, (and shape it as a poem) it usually gives you a better chance to 'get' something, for yourself, in your own way. This, your own way, may be more likely to become a permanent trait in you if you have looked at it deeply, focused on it, reflected upon it, and formed it into a particular shape (eg a poem). Shaping up a poem is therefore an incentive to you to look more deeply than usual, and to benefit from that.

The poem when shaped can be a reminder to you the writer, a stepping stone on your journey towards greater understanding. And it can be a different kind of stepping stone to the reader, a pointer for them towards an area that they too can look at more deeply for themselves.

While we can use the analogy of a journey very usefully, one of the risks is that it suggests the experience we need to 'get' ourselves is somehow 'out there'. This is often partially true (nature, flowers, beloved friends) but as we go further into all this, the distinction between 'out there' and 'in here' becomes less and less distinct. We start to realise that as we journey further the important stuff to 'get' is inside us – and only when we investigate our inner selves can we 'get' that which we need to 'get' in order to go further.

In sitting in anticipation of a potential poem we may be better able to realise these insights for ourselves than if we simply sit in contemplation. 'May' not 'will'. You will have to decide what works for you.

An example in detail

While it's fresh in my mind, here's an example of a poem that came to me a couple of days ago. How did this one work for me at this time? What was going on behind the scenes that led to the final form?

I'd travelled away to a small east coast seaside resort (English east coast!) in order to attend the birthday celebrations of an old friend. It was a reunion with old friends as well as a chance to meet new people. During the afternoon I'd wandered around and enjoyed seeing families on the beach, queues for the fish and chip shop, the Victorian funicular railway going up the cliff, and I'd enjoyed going out along the pier. From there I'd been able to observe surfers at close quarters, because the pier took me out into the sea right to the point where they were hanging about on their boards waiting for the right wave.

What surfers do is they bob about in the water, looking, in their black wet suits, rather like seals. If a suitable wave comes along, they paddle like mad and, hopefully, catch the wave, stand up, and ride it in.

The waves on this day were not big, and the surfers were mostly not very experienced. They were having fun though, and some were riding waves effectively enough. However others were missing waves, or, having caught waves, were then standing up and falling off. Great to watch from close by!

That evening the birthday event went well. People had a good time, old friendships were renewed, new ones made, and people performed songs and dances and read poems and did drumming in a perfect example of a traditional, family and local community event.

During the course of the evening, unexpectedly, I had three separate conversations about death and grieving.

Early in the evening I found myself talking to a woman, a stranger to me. Oddly, we soon found that we were distantly related by marriage, (several of my cousins live in that area) which was energising and fun. The conversation then found itself entering the territory of difficult life situations, and she took a risk, and started sharing with me about how her partner had died a few months before, unexpectedly. And how devastating that had been for her. And how grief continued to knock her about in the way that it does in these circumstances.

I listened as best I could, feeling very moved by her story, and by the privilege of hearing it from her in this way. Someone else's grief touches me, partly because it connects me back with my own. I felt very tender towards her because she was going through a lot of suffering, it was going to continue for a long time, and that was what she had to face.

And here we were at a party, where lots of people, including myself, were having a really good time. Ouch! That's one of the weird aspects of grieving. You're going through this enormous painful process, and life goes on around you as though everything is still normal.

Later in the evening, an old friend arrived, someone I had not seen for many years, not since we were young. In the intervening period, his partner, whom I had also known, had died after a long illness. As some of the details of her illness and dying and her courage in facing it all emerged into the space between us, we were both caught by grief and sadness and tears. Not surprising really – if you cannot cry over the death of someone you love, when can you cry? - but unexpected, perhaps because we were at a party, and our expectations at a party are of having a fun time.

Finally, when I got back to the hotel where some of us who were from far afield were staying, I sat in the bar for half an hour where three of the four other people (all older) had lost partners in the last few years. I had a conversation, particularly with one man, about the experience of grieving, and what had helped, and what hadn't, and the kinds of things that you go through.

In the morning, after a short, poor night's sleep, I sat in my hotel room and knew I had about half an hour before I had to go for breakfast. I thought I would sit, and see whether there was a poem that wanted to shape itself up at this time. While a lot had happened the day before, the conversations about death came up strongly for me. I remembered the first talk, where the woman had talked about 'waves of grief', and how when one wave had passed it was a question of waiting for the next one, and dealing with it as best you could.

The image of the surfers came into my mind and there was a connection in my mind between waves of grief (a metaphor), and the physical waves that surfers ride. It was one of those 'aha' moments, a moment of insight. I sat with this and let it develop. I saw how waves of grief are like physical waves: they just keep coming, and you have no control over them. I saw how it might be possible to learn to ride waves of grief like surfers learn to ride real waves. I felt that when we are engaged with grief over a long period then some people probably do manage to do that to some extent, while others don't. I had a series of strong images around all this, and then, with time pressing, I moved into letting words arise.

Initially something concrete came up like:

'I walked out along the pier and saw the surfers ride the waves' and then 'I stood on the ground while you told me of your waves of grief.'

It was looking like it could be a poem with a form that drew parallels between real waves and internal waves of grief.

But grief, from what I know and from what I'd heard the night before, is initially so powerful. I had images of really big waves and powerful surf, and words like 'pounded and battered in the surf'.

As I went through it all again and again, with the words I had, and referred back to my images also, I had a realisation that there is often a process to grief, and that was what seemed to be emerging in my poem. When death happens there is a storm of grief, which creates the waves, which initially pound us. Later they lose intensity. A lot later they lose more still, though we may still be affected from time to time.

I sense at this point that I have a poem with four parts and words along these lines:

1 Death drops in, storm of grief
2 pounded and battered in the surf
3 waiting for the next wave
4 occasional wave, reminder of someone you love.

But what about the pier and the surfers, and learning to surf – where do they fit in? The painful answer is that they don't, and that the integrity and impact of the poem that is emerging requires that I drop them entirely. I started there, but the poem has moved on and they don't figure in the final line-up. Maybe another time. How terrible I always find it to let go of something like this!

In the meantime, once that realisation comes, the rest of the poem comes together around the four part form. I go through it several times and this is what emerges, and this is what I quickly note down:

When, over the horizon,
Death drops in on someone we love
it creates a storm of grief.

At first we are pounded and battered
by continual huge waves

that toss us in the surf like a rag doll
so that we know we are dying too.

Later the energy subsides a little
and we are just waiting for the next wave
to roll us over and swamp us for a while.

A lot later we may even learn to welcome
the occasional rogue wave of sadness
a memento of someone we loved
and of how much we loved them.

I'm happy enough with this. It tells a truth of my experience (and as far as I can tell, of others' experience). It's pretty readable and clear. It fits with my values, for while it deals with suffering it offers a potential way through, and shows how the power of your love is reflected in the power of the grief.

I can also see how the surfer angle would have detracted from the clarity of this poem in this form. So, OK, there's something that works better here without that bit. I can see that.

While I'm happy enough, I don't feel I've completely nailed it, but then I've learned to let that be. At this stage it's much too early to come to any judgement. Poems grow in our awareness as time passes. This is a new-born poem. Initial responses are often wildly out, one way or the other. Often I have a sense of 'that's not really even a poem' and later realise that of course it very much is a poem.

There will be an editing phase later, but in the meantime, I can go off to breakfast.

(In fact, when I type it up later, I leave it as it is. The phrase 'like a rag doll' continues to niggle at me. Is it too close to a cliché or does it serve the purpose? For the time being I leave it. The poem as a whole is good enough for me. It speaks to that moment.)

Queries on shaping a form

I've tried holding the beginning poem in my mind but I just want to write down any bits I've got straight away. I don't want to wait.

You could experiment. You could try not waiting and see what happens. You could try holding beyond what feels comfortable and see what happens. You could try bringing out 'the one who doesn't want to wait' more fully and engage in dialogue with them. What is it they want actually? Is there any way they can get it in some other part of your life and leave this part (the poetry part) to you and your 'more patient one?'

I think I can hold a poem in my mind, but not a long one.

You may be correct, but you may surprise yourself. You may also be able to develop your ability over time.

Sometimes I can be surprised at how long a poem turns out to be. I have held it in my mind while it forms. It doesn't feel difficult to do that, and I feel a strong connection with all elements of the poem and the way they come together as a whole. And then when I write it out I'm surprised at just how many square inches of page space it takes up. It didn't feel like that in my mind.

Step 8 Writing down

At some point when you're ready, or often when you don't feel ready but it can't wait any longer, write it down on the page. Don't fuss too much at this stage. Just get it down as a whole. You can refine it more when you come to the next stage. If the other parts of the process have done their thing it usually doesn't take long. This part often takes me no more than ten minutes, sometimes a lot less.

If that's how it is for you also, then you can enjoy the sense of flow and connection.

However don't worry if it takes longer, or if it doesn't flow. That's the way it is sometimes.

When this happens to me it might be because I thought I had the poem clear in my mind but discover that actually I don't. Or maybe time pressures (got to get up for work/that meeting/the train) mean I'm pushing myself because if I don't push, the whole thing might be lost.

There are two choices at this point. One is to re-enter briefly the inner experience and check with that reality. Sometimes that is enough to enable the blockage to clear and the words to flow. The other way is just to keep going. Maybe you feel you don't have time to check back. Maybe you can't reconnect with that space at this moment. Maybe it feels as though there is too much being held in your mind and you want to get whatever is there down while it's still there as a whole.

If you keep going then, if you're like me, there may be crossings out, substituted bits, crossings out of the substituted bits, arrows that move bits around, all done quickly.

When that is happening to me I usually aim to keep going. Something is better than nothing. I can edit later.

Momentum is all. If I pause too long then I may never restart.

It's like I imagine a water-colourist feels: can't hang around here, the paint is drying...

It's like when I've mixed a load of cement and I'm laying some slabs: no time to hang around searching down the garden for the exact right slab and wondering if the colour is right and oh, isn't that a pretty rose over there... the cement is going off (technical phrase for setting harder!) all the time and the job has to be done NOW.

Actually this analogy works pretty well in other ways too. The slab laying, like the writing down, is only a short late phase in the whole process. I have to plan the shape of the work in my mind, assemble all the materials and tools, make the preparations, and then go, go, go. For a recent piece of slab laying I'd spent months thinking about it (off and on you understand), then a day and a half preparing the ground, and getting everything ready. The actual laying of the slabs took only an (intense) hour, and mortaring the gaps between them another (intense) hour. Then I was done.

Apart from recovering, and then slowly clearing everything away.

So if you find yourself struggling in the writing down phase treat it as a learning experience and keep going one way or the other. Try to respect whatever internal forces are making things difficult, while insisting at this moment on continuing.

Other ways?

As I've explained previously, in this method the poem is already effectively 'written' before you write it down.

This may be a very different approach to the way you think poetry should be written, or is written, or the way you usually write poetry if you already do it. What is your normal way (if you have one)? Pause a moment and reflect upon that. How do you actually write poetry?

And if you don't write yourself (or even if you do), how do you think 'regular' poets write? How do they do it? What is their method?

I don't actually know the answer to those last three questions. In my more surreal moments, I imagine that regular poets pick up a pen after a moment of inspiration and write a couple of lines. Then they pause and look into the distance, thinking, and feeling. Then they scrawl out a couple more lines (with their quill pen...). Then more pauses and looking into the distance. And so on.

Then they go through it scratching things out and writing better things in till they can't see what is what, and have to write the whole thing out again. Then some more blood, sweat and tears, followed by sloughs of despond and crests of confidence as to whether it's any good as a poem.

My imagination may be pure fantasy. Or not...

Queries on writing down
What about writing straight to computer?

Whatever works for you. I'm hampered by the two-finger typing method ('look and peck') and by being an old-fashioned guy who grew up in the days of pens and paper and still likes them for some purposes. (When I was seven and we first learned to write in ink at school, we used a nib pen that we dipped into an inkwell in the corner of the desk...) If you have the requisite speed and the liking for it, then typing straight to computer is what is right for you. The technicality is not what counts. Only the poetry counts. Well, maybe Reality counts more…

How do I know when it's time to start writing down, and when to leave it longer?

Let's look at it first from the outside and assume there are three possible points to start writing down: too early, just right, and too late.

Now sometimes these points are clearly apparent to you from the inside (that is, when you're in the middle of shaping a poem). You know when you're approaching the writing down time, you're clear about it, you're relaxed, you know there's a broad window for the 'right' time, you know when you haven't reached it yet, and you know when you have. And then you write down.

And sometimes it's really quite messy, and you just don't know. That's how it is. Unfortunately this is something you just get to know your way around by experience, and by making those things sometimes called mistakes, but which we'll refer to here as, oh I don't know, what about cogent learning opportunities?

Here are some clues. If it's too early, then it might not feel right, or the words won't come easily, or you have a sense of something missing. Now these might just be negative messages from your inner critic, and you need to carry on anyway. (We look at the critic in Section 3.) Or you might decide to listen to these feelings and go back to the experience and continue the shaping process. If that works, then you were right to go back.

It's also possible to leave it too long. You delay and delay because you're convinced it's not really there yet, and then you discover that you have 'gone off the boil', that you've got side-tracked into other stuff, and that the essence of what you had has faded, and that you are not able to re-access it. Ouch!

It does happen. It's happened to me. We are dealing with the volatility of our energy and attention here. It's not infinitely flexible, and it's not under our control. We're riding a wave, and the wave comes to an end at some point.

When I'm shaping a poem, then for maybe twenty-five per cent of the time, I'm really clear about the time to write down. The other times it's not clear. I've learned to wait at times, but at other times I've learned to do it anyway, even if I don't feel ready. Perhaps I have a good outline and form, but there are some parts of the poem that are vague or unfinished. I don't feel completely ready, but experience has told me that this is when I have to do it anyway.

I have a phrase for this point: 'this is as good as it's going to get'. I know I'm not perfectly prepared but waiting longer will not improve matters. In fact waiting longer will make things worse. Because I will be losing energy and focus. This is as good as it's going to get – time to write it down. I'm going to trust that I have done enough preparing, and that the writing down process will fill in the gaps.

So, faced with this dilemma and uncertainty, let yourself get hold of your notebook or laptop. Get hold of it with trepidation, or doubt, or fear, or bravado, or relief, or determination. But get hold of it anyway, and then find that writing down is what happens next.

You are the only one who can get to know your own body, energy levels, capacity for concentration in sufficient detail to know when is the time to wait longer, and when is the time to write-down, now. As in the childhood game of 'hide and seek' – 'Coming, ready or not!'

I don't like my words when I'm writing. I keep thinking 'this isn't a poem.'

Keep going anyway. This is almost certainly the critic speaking, and at this stage, if you can, simply ignore the voice. Or say to yourself (your inner critic), 'Maybe it isn't. I'll just write this stuff down anyway.' I think I could probably collect together a whole book of poems that were originally labelled 'this isn't a poem' as I was writing them down. They were poems.

Another way to handle this is to consider that there is a potential element of truth in this comment if we extend it slightly: 'This isn't a poem like I think a poem is supposed to be...' Maybe it's a kind of poem that is new to you, new to the world. Hold your nerve and continue. The world needs new kinds of poems it hasn't seen before.

Step 9 Immediate editing

At some stage, usually quite soon, it's useful to make a fair copy of your poem and make some adjustments to it.

You may do the original write-down by hand and then transfer the poem to a computer a bit later.

You may already have it on computer, or you may prefer to keep everything hand-written. Your choice!

Let's remind ourselves of a couple of points I made previously:

At this stage you can make a few adjustments or amendments to make it (a) more truthful, or (b) more comprehensible.

There's an important distinction between those kinds of edits and a wholesale re-write. You're too close to the poem at this stage to know what it truly is, what this new creation really is that you've given life to. You can't know what is 'good' or 'not good'. Trust in the model, trust in your inner process, trust in the poem, and let it be as it is now for a good long while.

And here are a couple of extra points:

One simple editing process that I sometimes finding myself trying is flipping the person. I may have written it in the 1st person ('I' or 'we'), but realise it needs to be in 2nd ('you') or 3rd ('she', 'he' or 'they' for example), or needs to be from an impersonal perspective. Sometimes the meaning becomes clearer if I make that adjustment.

Another simple flip is the tense. Usually this involves moving it from the past tense to the present. Writing in the present tense has more immediacy. This may capture the moment more vividly.

At this point in the process, once I've typed the poem out, I usually like to date it and then write a few notes about how it came to be, and any obvious connections with what's been happening in my life. Sometimes I write a few general diary type notes as well, because I don't keep a diary but do like to have a reminder of goings-on in my life...

What customs do you have, or what customs will you develop for yourself?

Queries on immediate editing

If I do hand-write it down, is it OK to leave a gap between first writing down and then transferring to laptop?

The advantage of having only a small gap (within the hour, say) is that you are still fresh with the experience of shaping the poem, and you bring that freshness to the typing up, and the small edits that happen at that time. You maintain perhaps, more of the 'wholeness' of the experience and the poem.

There's also the simple pleasure of seeing your poem take shape on the page in front of your eyes. Why delay on that?

However, sometimes needs must. Life gets in the way, or work, or children. In a busy schedule poetry might have to squeeze in around the edges, and only just fit. Type it up to computer when you can. There's sometimes a great pleasure for me, if the typing is delayed, in seeing how the poem took me in a surprising direction, which in the intervening period I had kind of forgotten.

The other option, I must add in, is that you may be the kind of person who doesn't do laptops or computers. They are not a requirement. They do make editing and amending amazingly easy, and they make sharing the poems with others available at the touch of a few buttons. For most people they are the obvious route. But they are not a requirement. Making a fair copy by hand and placing it in a hand-made beautiful binder, or giving it to a friend on hand-made paper may be your style. Good for you. I salute you. I'd love to get something like that. (And I loved it when I did get something like that.)

An example: Renewal

Here's an example of some editing I did recently. Curiously, the poem had been written five months before, and then forgotten (poor thing) in an old notebook.

The poem came, as usual, out of a session of sitting in meditation, and draws parallels between two current 'outer' work projects and the ongoing 'inner' work project of meditation. It finishes with a response to all of this.

Here's how it was noted down in my notebook. When I scrawl something down I'm usually writing really fast while it's still in my mind. It's not necessarily clear where the ends of the lines are for poetic reasons, and where there is simply not enough room on the page of my notebook. I don't bother too much because I know that's something I can easily sort out on first editing when, in any case, it's easier to see what it's like on the printed page. What you see here is pretty well what was in my notebook (though much more legible, obviously!).

There were some amendments I made while I wrote it out. Some quick strikethroughs of words or phrase and then something different put in, plus a couple of inserted additional phrases. I usually do most of these as I go along. I'd say the number here is not atypical for me, but on average slightly on the high side in terms of numbers of adjustments in the writing down phase.

Renewal

My hands ~~dig~~ wield the fork, dig out ~~weeds~~
stones
from the bank and many ~~stones~~ weeds
shake the soil from their roots
~~My hands and eyes~~ use the big stones
to rebuild the retaining wall
holding the garden back from the field.

My fingers click the keys
dig out pages from my website and
delete them
I ~~form~~ write new pages, insert images, rebuild
~~a renewed different~~ the site.

My meditating mind ~~digs out~~ sees old
patterns
~~from~~ form in my mind, digs them out, holds
them to the
light, shakes them a little
watches ~~the~~ some soil trickle down
lets them go where they will in
their renewed form.

Some part of me laughs with
delight at it all.

    As I typed it out I realised I wanted to make a lot of
the lines shorter so that the sense became clearer. So
the first line became
    'My hands wield the fork'
    But then when I'd got the whole thing typed, I saw
how if I put 'My hands' as the first line, then the rest of

the stanza had a repeating pattern or list that followed from that, and moreover, that I could repeat that pattern with the other stanzas. The first lines of the stanzas then become 'My hands', My fingers,' and 'My meditating mind'.   That felt clearer, more satisfying, and right. It should make it easier for the parallels to be apparent. I see how I can also make the first line of the final stanza into 'Some part of me' to fit the same pattern.

This meant changing 'I write new pages' in stanza 2 to 'write new pages' to fit the pattern. No problem there, the essential meaning remains the same.

There were one or two other minor changes – for example I added 'old' in stanza 2 because that felt a little clearer.

And then the whole poem looks like this:

Renewal

My hands
wield the fork
dig out stones from the bank
dig out many weeds
shake the soil from their roots
use the big stones to rebuild the retaining wall
holding the garden back from the field.

My fingers
click the keys
dig out old pages from my website
delete them
write new pages
insert images
rebuild the site.

My meditating mind
sees old patterns form in my mind
digs them out
holds them to the light
shakes them a little
watches some soil trickle down
lets them go where they will
in their renewed form.

Some part of me
laughs with delight at it all.

I'm happy with it. I like the last stanza which catches me by surprise even when I remember it's there. Some part of me still laughs with delight at it all.

Step 10 Later editing

Over the next few days, weeks or months of maturation and life, come back to the poem and see it with fresh eyes: more as a reader, less as a writer. Maybe make some changes, some improvements. At this stage you can get a trusted friend or two to read it and give you feedback as to where it works for them or where it's not clear. Make changes as you see fit. Almost always these changes will be relatively minor.

Why will they be relatively minor? Why aren't wholesale re-writes necessarily the best thing here?

Because what we're aiming to do here is capture the essence of your connections with your deeper being. These connections, by their nature, are not part of your everyday life. If you come along later and make a lot of radical changes, there is a risk that those changes will be coming from your everyday self. You will be diluting the essence of the deeper experience.

This may be particularly the case if the insights you gained are challenging to your everyday self. There will be a tendency to water those insights down, and make the poem fit more with your normal self, and normal life. What a loss that would be!

Whenever you consider making changes, try to connect them back to the original impetus for the poem. If necessary, close your eyes and recapture as well as you can that experience. Ask yourself, are the amendments I'm thinking of still true to that connection, that event?

If you do feel a big urge to re-write, you could, instead, actually do a re-write. Sit down and contemplate the same topic again, allow new words to arise, and shape up a new poem. And then do it again...

We can think of a parallel with painting. We're looking for the immediacy of water-colour, not the

93

protracted layering of oil paints. Nothing wrong with oils, just a different mode for a different perspective.

Nothing wrong with wholesale re-writes of poems over a long period. Just a different mode, for a different purpose.

What a trusted friend can do for you

I have a great friend, Trevor, who offers me wonderfully supportive, sensitive and sometimes challenging criticism. I listen with closeness to his responses and often implement amendments based on his insights - probably about three quarters of the time. Everyone should have a Trevor – but you can't have mine, he's taken!

If you're interested in recruiting someone to take this role for you, or if you may be interested in taking on this role for someone else, these are some of the qualities that Trevor brings to our meetings:

He likes poetry. Pretty important, but not everyone does.

He's read and studied poetry widely in his life and has a great feel for the tradition. I trust his knowledge and his approach.

He has pursued his own inner life journey, and is therefore familiar with some of the approaches I take to working with those inner energies: both the creative, life-affirming energies, and the critical, contracting ones; and the ways they might manifest in my poetry.

He has also pursued a spiritual path, in a variety of guises. He has a familiarity with the broad territory and the potential routes through it.

He's interested in the phenomena of deeper inner states, has experienced connections with them in himself, and has reflected persistently about them.

When he reads my poems he does so closely, with attention to detail. He connects with them. I can feel this when he talks to me about them. When he talks to me about them in this way I get a very strong affirmation that my poems are 'real' and that so am I, and so is he.

He tells me where he doesn't understand what I'm trying to say. This often leads to some wonderful discussions where we really get into the detail of what happened, what I made of it, what it means, and what I can say about it. We don't always agree at the end, but we certainly know a lot more about it all.

He tells me where he does understand what I'm saying but thinks I could say it better. Ditto in terms of follow-up discussions.

He says when he likes a poem (most of the time), and, occasionally, when he doesn't. I'm becoming familiar with which poems he might not like and so I look forward to teasing him a little with them...

He doesn't tell me which poems are 'good' or 'not good' in the sense of comparing them to others and finding them acceptable or not according to whatever rules of poetry-judging they are supposed to fit in with.

He tells me where certain words or phrases don't work for him. This kind of feedback is like gold-dust to me. As the writer, (and then a reader) I have the original experience to refer to. As a reader without the original experience, Trevor can help me fine-tune my words more accurately.

He sometimes questions my interpretations of whatever experience I am writing about and describing. Once we've looked at this in more detail, considered the various options, mulled it over in the light of different traditions and perspectives then I find myself very reassured. Either I'm going to make some adjustments in the light of what we've discussed, or I'm affirmed in my original take on it. I like to be accurate if I'm bringing in references to Buddhist, Christian or other areas of knowledge. The challenges test out what I'm saying.

Step11 Sharing

Sharing: why it's probably a good thing, but when and how are important

As we said before: when the time is right, you may want to let your poem out into the world in some way. Make it available to others, even if only to your future self. Keep it moving, circulate the love!

OK, first things first: you don't have to share it with anyone, ever. You can keep it secret to your bosom as long as you like and if necessary for ever. That's the basis on which you can enable yourself to write the difficult things that you don't want to write. You know, those difficult things you don't want to write, but which are really important if you do write them.

They're important because the stuff we're reluctant to face/admit/deal with/open to is almost always crucial stuff that we have to face/admit/deal with/open to if we're going to be able to move on.

However it's only if we are confident that we have total control that we can usually manage to bring that into the open. So we tell ourselves that if we write it down, it doesn't ever have to see the public light of day – and we mean it. We seriously mean it!

Later on, we know we may (and in my experience usually do) change our minds. It's amazing what at first seems mind-blowingly shocking and confessional becomes acceptable, interesting and even slightly ordinary after it has had a bit of fresh air blowing over it for a while. Our capacity to surround something (anything!) with a solid shell of shame, guilt and fear is pretty extraordinary.

But the first thing to reassure ourselves with is that stuff coming up to us from deep in our beings is still in our control when it emerges into the light of day. It need go no further.

We can also recognise that our future self may be the 'other' we need to communicate with most. When we come back to a poem after some time, part of us is reading it from the outside. We may be grateful to our past self for shaping this poem – and for sharing it with us now.

And sometimes we're very happy with our poem. We want to share it. We want other people to share in the joy of our experience and the joy of our insight.

And sometimes we're not sure. To share or not to share, that is the question. To go public or not to go public?

To help tip the balance one way or the other, or to help determine whether to do so now or later, here is a summary of some of the issues to consider.

Reasons to say 'no' or 'not yet'

We need to leave the poem to mature.

This can take months. You come back to the poem at different times and you see, because you are not so very close to the experience, where it needs to be clearer. You may also see where it doesn't quite fit with your values, or your truth. Leave it a while, and let it develop. Otherwise you risk releasing a version of the poem that you want to change later, and that can be difficult. Once it's out in the world, it may develop a life of its own.

Our motivation is suspect.

We might check out with ourselves: 'What is my current relationship with the desire for wealth, fame, and approval?'

If we've been honest with ourselves we will have been aware of these longings for some time, and will have been attempting to reach a negotiated settlement with them. However they are powerful forces. They may be back in control, or hold the balance of power, and tip us into doing some actions that aren't necessarily in our best interests or that of the world we are trying to serve.

As always the key to managing these longings is conscious awareness. Make your choice with as much freedom as you can. If you decide to go for wealth and fame, do it as an active choice, from which you can also turn aside at any point if you wish.

This makes me too vulnerable.

It's liberating to be in touch with, and express, aspects of ourselves that we've felt obliged to keep hidden. Wow, how good can that feel! Sometimes we want to tell the world everything in the first flush of that new found freedom. Sometimes that is too soon. It may be better to wait and really check out how this new place feels, and the extent to which you want to share it more widely.

The world is not yet ready.

Sometimes you are ready, but the world isn't. If your friends, acquaintances, neighbours, and the strangers down the street know xxxx about you, or about the way you think, feel, or behave, they may not like it. And that dislike may turn to outrage over certain issues. Be realistic, and be prepared. It's OK to say, 'No, I think this stuff has to wait till later.'

Reasons to say 'yes'

This is just who I am

The poem is simply an extension of yourself and who you are. You're perfectly happy with yourself and your poem. There's no reason not to share it. It's just like talking to a bunch of friends telling them how you are, or putting a post on Facebook. It's no big deal.

Of benefit to others

So, you've written a really insightful, original, feelingful, truthful poem. If other people read it they will pick up on those qualities, and that insight. It will affect them in a good way. It will bring benefit to them. In some way, probably small, but maybe large, it will affect their lives for the better. It's important to get it out there so they have the chance. If they can't read it they can't benefit.

Share or get sick

This is an insight from Ken Wilber. He says there's a kind of cosmic rule at play here. The deal is this: if you are granted glimpses of enlightenment, or insights into the nature of reality, it's so you can share them. If you don't share them – if for reasons of selfishness or fear or sloth you fail to share what you've been given, you'll get sick. This is not some kind of divine punishment thing; it's just the way these things work. Think of blood, or air, or food. You have to keep them circulating or they go bad. If you try and hold on to and live off a particular bit of blood or air or food, it won't work. They go bad, you get sick. If you've been granted insight, give it the opportunity to keep circulating. Or (said in suitable (US) southern accent) you get sick as a d-o-o-o-g.

Truth, and shifts in the balance of power

When you, in the privacy of your room, delve into your being and come up with insights into how you have kept parts of yourself hidden, and then translate those insights into a poem, you shift the balance of power within yourself. You are more vulnerable but curiously more powerful. You have brought the energy back from where it was tied up in keeping things hidden to where it is part of you in plain sight of yourself.

If you decide to share that poem more widely you amplify that process of power reclamation. You are saying confidently, 'This is who I am. I used to be afraid of you over there (that is, whoever or whatever you had vested the power in) but now I'm not. I'm who I am.' When you do this the balance of power in the world also shifts a little between those forces of openness and vulnerability, and those forces of fear, dishonesty and suppression.

You may be an inspiration to others

Truth, courage, and openness are contagious. When other people read poems you have written which incorporate those qualities they will catch the bug. It may be uncomfortable for them – they will be made to face up to where they are being less than honest and truthful with themselves. But discomfort is inevitable in a process of change. It is almost always the first step (and often the second, third and fourth too).

If they get the bug, they may be inspired to go further down their own path of discovery and exploration (within or without). They may even decide to express the results of their journeyings through the medium of poetry.

Validate the inner path

A lot of modern culture emphasises and rewards work in the 'outer' world. What has been achieved in the material world is simply extraordinary. We all benefit in innumerable ways. I'm happy to join in with the celebration.

But the 'inner' way has its own validity. If you put your poem about the depth of your being out into the world it is like adding a single stone to a cairn on the way up a mountain. It's a long way short of building a skyscraper, but one day who knows what will emerge from our collective efforts?

We need a certain challenge

We need to keep challenging ourselves (to the right degree) or we stop moving and instead stagnate. Putting your stuff out there may feel a little challenging to do. It should. You may have to overcome some reluctance. That's good. All sorts of inner critics will tell you not to, and offer cogent reasons. Hold your nerve and do it anyway.

If we are growing and developing then we always have a growing edge. Sometimes excitement takes us beyond ourselves. Sometimes fear holds us back. Often there's a bit of a see-sawing motion back and forth over the edge while we get used to the new territory. Putting your poems out into the world will be no different in this respect.

As ever, notice what happens. Do it with awareness. See what you are learning.

Avoid false modesty

Perhaps you are a conscientious person. You try to do what's right. You know perhaps that blowing your own trumpet and, in effect, shouting 'Look at me!' is undesirable, ill-mannered, and unseemly. In order to avoid this you may err on the side of caution and not risk being egotistical. You keep your poems to yourself. 'Probably they are not good enough,' you say to yourself. 'But even if they are good enough, best not to show off by putting them forward.'

Sorry, falsely-modest people, but that's 'not good enough'. There's no escape in playing safe. Underestimating your value is as damaging to yourself, and as much of a loss to the world, as overestimating your value. There's no escape in false modesty. It's a waste. That's the way it is. You have to be as realistic as you can, and then go for it on that basis. If you want to grow and develop, that is.

If you want to stagnate and not fulfil your potential, well, that's your choice. In that case you can be as falsely modest as you like.

Keep the channel open

And finally here's a great piece of wisdom from someone who clearly knew and understood. I had this pinned to our notice board for a long time. It's from Martha Graham, a woman who was a dancer and teacher, and who said this:

'There is a vitality, a life force, an energy, a quickening that is translated through you into action, and because there is only one of you in all of time, this expression is unique. And if you block it, it will never exist through any other medium and it will be lost. The world will not have it. It is not your business to determine how good it is nor how valuable nor how it compares with other expressions. It is your business to keep it yours clearly and directly, to keep the channel open. You do not even have to believe in yourself or your work. You have to keep yourself open and aware to the urges that motivate you. Keep the channel open...'

It's not the same as 'getting published'

Really not the same. My understanding is that in what we might call conventional literary poetry circles, there is an emphasis on 'getting published'. That is, published usually in various poetry magazines. These magazines emphasise that they will only publish previously unpublished poems. So if you are a poet who wants to get published, you can't release any poem, not even on to your website, or else it will be disqualified from ever being published.

One poet I read described how he might send a batch of ten poems to a magazine. Most, if not all, come back after a while as unsuitable. He then sends them to another potential magazine (or competition, or book publisher or whatever). And so on. He mentioned, almost in passing, that at any one time he might have two hundred poems circulating in this way. Two hundred.

Multiply that number by however many poets there are trying to access published outlets and you have an awful lot of poems circulating through the ether, unread except by a few editors (who are presumably overwhelmed by massive numbers of poems).

If you're a poet in this mode, when do you decide a poem is never going to be published and therefore you could for example put it up on your website? When it's been turned down by every magazine in existence? Presumably not, because once it's been through every magazine then various editors will have changed, or they might have forgotten your poem, so you could try again!

Even if you decide it's the end of the line for a particular poem it's hard to put it up on your site even then, because it advertises itself to the world as a poem that has been turned down as not good enough to be published by every single poetry magazine in existence! And that you have written a poem turned down by every single poetry magazine in existence! Who would do that?

I ask you: Is that a sane system? Or a dumb-ass system? You decide.

In what ways might I share my poems?

Send them to friends, put one in your email signature, send them to local newsletters, have a website, make a book, send them to specialist websites. Invite your friends for supper and tell them there will be two poems with each course.

Feel your way into it. What is right for me at this moment? What is right for this poem? How might this poem serve the world in even the smallest way?

Sit with 'sharing my poems' as your topic. See what comes up. Write a poem about it. Share that one.

Leave one in a telephone box. Post one to your biggest enemy with an apology. Send one with a message of support for the prime minister. (Tough job for anyone. Need whatever inspiration they can get...)

The universe is infinite and there are an infinite number of ways to share your poems. Avoid artificial restrictions.

Postscript to Section 2: Asking for help

At one stage or another in the whole process you might like to ask for help. Depending on your values and/or your inner path, this might be, for example, from your Higher Self, or the Buddha, or Big Mind, or God, or your Authentic Self, or the cosmos in general. The purpose of this is:

(a) often it really does help. Accessing your deeper parts and shaping up poems can be a difficult process to do and we can use all the help available

(b) it helps to edge us towards that place where what we are doing is not just from and for ourselves but transcending that

I currently have a small group of figures that I call on from time to time, depending on the circumstances, and where I'm at in my life. They have these qualities in common:

- they are wholly benevolent
- I trust them
- they are full of wisdom
- they call me on my shortcomings but in a humorous and loving way
- they often tell me just to get on with it and that I'm doing fine

When I bring them into the picture it's sometimes because I have some big topic to contemplate and express and I'm feeling particularly inadequate to handling it. I'm looking for support to go on (or counsel to wait longer) and clues as to how to go about it.

But often it's because I'm stuck, or unsure, and I'm in the middle of something. I may be at the stage where I'm feeling my way towards a topic to contemplate and can't find one. I may be unsure about the kind of approach I could take. I may be unclear about the form, or the ending, or whether it's time to move on, or stay with it longer.

So I just pause and take a step back from wherever I am, without losing whatever level of clarity I'm enjoying, and then I ask. Sometimes it's just a silent sense of wanting help, with a sense of who I'm asking. Sometimes it's a specific question to a named figure: 'Dear Buddha, please help me here. I've lost track of what I could do for the best with this poem.' There are lots of images of the Buddha so I am usually visualising a Buddha-like image. With God, I just have a bodily sense of the warmest, most loving presence. It's easy to ask him anything. With my three wise guys, I see them sitting in a half-circle around me, like they're my best mates, except they know a lot more than any of my friends (wonderful though they are). With them it's interesting, because they all have a slightly different take on things, so I get a rounded view.

So, I ask for help, and then I sit back and wait. And I get responses. And I take the hint, or the advice, or whatever, and I apply it. And then I'm grateful and give thanks.

Here's an example.

How to enjoy the voices of contraction

The voices of contraction may be very loud.
Round the table confusion reigns.
In the democracy of your being
fear and neediness may carry the majority vote.

Invite the Buddha to the table.
He may say nothing but his presence brings calm.
From that space the way forward becomes clear.

Even the voices of contraction may start to sing.

And here's a note I wrote at the time which explains a little of the process:

'this one was interesting. Came from notes I wrote a couple of weeks ago (following a 'difficult' meeting...). Returned to it this morning, and sat with it all a long time, while the shape and the meaning 'failed' to coalesce. Finally got the sense of the Buddha, asked him for wisdom on the poem, and what to do (my fear was contracting me...). Listened to that calm voice, then realised he needed to come into the poem (more fear...). Sat down with little idea still of what to say, and this emerged. Much shorter than I expected. Woke at 5.15, started to write at (?) 7.30. Now 8am.'

Resistance to guides

Now you will have to find your own way through all this. Maybe you already have helpers you go to. Maybe you feel you don't need them. Maybe the idea of internal wise figures that you dialogue with is alien to you. Maybe your rational mind is kicking in and saying, 'Now hang on a minute...'

I'm with you there. I've been there a lot. I still find it strange.

How does it work? (Because for many people it really does.) I don't know. I have theories. There's a whole subject area and discussion here around what this all means and how to interpret it, but it's beyond the scope of this book (though see below for a little bit more on it).

My suggestion is that if you already have a habit of asking for help, you continue to do so, and notice whether and how it develops. And if you don't have a practice in this way that you consider experimenting with it, and notice what happens – both in terms of your poetry and in terms of yourself.

Asking for help nudges us beyond the everyday

The other benefit from asking for help from these 'wise' figures is that when we ask for their help, we start to get a perspective that is beyond our own current one. We already do our best, but we mostly live in the everyday world. That has a powerful influence, and shapes our thinking, our feelings, and our interpretations of what is happening more than we probably like to believe.

When we get into a clearer space through meditation (or some other method) then we start to get a perspective that is beyond the ordinary. From there the world looks, feels, and (depending on your philosophical bent) is different.

Shaping a poem from that space helps us to become more familiar and at ease with that new perspective. When we ask for help from those figures, one way of describing what we are doing is to say that we are accessing within us a deeper view of the world – a view from beyond where we normally are. We ask for help, and the help we get is from beyond our habitual patterns. We probably like it, because that's what we are trying to access, but it will also feel strange. It is strange, because to us at this moment it is the unknown. Later on it when it becomes more familiar, a new edge to the (new) unknown is formed, and we start the process all over.

Section 3 Barriers
Critics, Shadows, and Eccentricities

This is a crucial topic. In the previous section I provided you with all the detailed information you need to shape up poems from deep within you. Perhaps you have already had success in trying out the method – I hope so. However, as with any new process that you are learning, it's all fine till it goes wrong in some way. And, as with any new process, it will go wrong in some way, at some point.

Perhaps that's why this section may be the most crucial in the book.

Because this is the place where, if you don't handle it right, you will be blocked. Your poetry will be blocked. Either, you will be unable to write, or you may still be writing stuff but it will be dead. There will be no life there. You will be going through the motions.

This feels really bad.

That's because it is really bad.

If you've known the joy of connection and flow and aliveness translating into deep poetry then to be cut off from that is extremely painful. It hurts a lot.

The relatively good news is that:

- it's a common process that all of us go through in our lives
- there are skilful ways of handling it that you can learn about and develop
- when you do handle these barriers skilfully they are a source of tremendous energy and insight, which can do wonders for your poetic expression

We're going to come back to the skilful ways in a little bit and examine them in detail. However first we need to tease apart the different kind of barriers that can impact on us, then have a look at how barriers manifest (because sometimes it's not obvious what's happening), and then explain how we might at first use habitual methods of dealing with the situation that aren't actually that helpful.

Barriers to expect

I'm concentrating on inner barriers here. There can be what we call external, in-the-world barriers (for example, shortages of time, money, space, computers, pencils...) but I'm not dealing with those directly in this book. That's with you. (Actually, those external barriers are connected in various ways to our inner world, and the barriers may be more susceptible, long-term, to inner solutions, than to outer ones.)

Barriers can impact on us during all stages of the poetry-shaping process, including before we write, and therefore affecting whether we write at all, and afterwards, when we consider whether to share our work.

I'm going to divide these barriers into three broad kinds which I'm calling:
- 1 Critics, 2 Shadows, and 3 Eccentricities.

These correspond, in other language, to:
- known, dimly known, and unknown, or:
- conscious, sub-conscious, and unconscious.

Dividing barriers into these three types is cutting up what is in effect a spectrum into three. There are not necessarily clear boundaries between them. They shade into each other. We could divide the spectrum in other ways but for the purposes of our current work and understanding, then three is a convenient number. This is a map, not the territory.

How will these three kinds of barriers manifest in us in relation to our quest to write poetry? What will they feel like? How will we know they are there?

I'll take each of them in turn briefly.

Critics

Those barriers which are known to us usually take the form of critical inner voices.

Below is a sample list, not an exhaustive list, of the kind of comments our inner critical voices may make. Our barriers arise from within us and are therefore uniquely tuned to our individual beings. However here are some common ones:

- I can't do this
- Who do I think I am to write anything?
- I'm not good enough
- This isn't a poem
- I'm not a proper poet
- Nobody will like them
- People will laugh at me

(This is a terrible list to write. I'm feeling them all at once now. I can't go on writing this...)

These critical voices usually bring some degree of pain and suffering with them. But the pain is useful because we know through the pain that the voices are there. They are not hidden. They are, more or less, in the open. We know that they are there and what they are like. That's the good news because in that case we can start to work with them.

Shadows

When we feel a certain kind of resistance to writing poems, or a reluctance, or a blockage, then the likelihood is that we are dealing with shadows. If we feel uncomfortable around certain topics and don't want to look at them in depth, don't want to write poems about them, or just can't get near them somehow, then we are probably dealing with shadow material. We know dimly that something is wrong, or not working, but we can't articulate it, or explain it. We probably feel confusion around it. Nothing quite makes sense, and yet we can't get past it.

For various reasons, usually to do with childhood experiences, we have pushed these difficulties below the surface. They remain there out of sight, but affecting us. We do know something is wrong, but we don't know what it is.

The first step to take in handling shadow material is to start to bring it out into the open. Until that happens, we can't work with it.

Eccentricities

Sometimes difficult stuff is so deeply buried within us that we don't have any idea it's there. As far as we are concerned we are completely normal, regular people. It's those guys over there who are the weirdoes.

The main problem with eccentricities, with stuff that is so deeply buried that we don't know it's there… is that we don't know it's there. If we don't know it's there we can't start to bring it out into the open and therefore begin to work with it. It will, unbeknown to us, affect all our relations, including relations with our meditation and our poetry.

There are two main sources of clues about the existence of eccentricities and they both involve other people.

When we see things in other people that we find difficult, or which bring up strong feelings in us, then that could be a clue about material hidden in ourselves.

And other people, if they are relatively clear, can see things in us that we can't see in ourselves. If we're able to trust them, then we might learn from them.

Other names for what I'm calling eccentricities, (in an effort to be kind and relatively positive) might include weirdnesses, kinks, neuroses, trouble, difficulties, and obsessions.

The 'rule' about barriers

There's a 'rule' about groups and group dynamics that I like to quote when I'm talking about groups:

'The first rule of groups is that conflict will arise. Handle it well and it will be a creative process. Handle it badly and it will be destructive.'

We can adapt this for writing poetry from a deeper place:

'The first rule of writing poetry from a deeper place is that barriers will arise. Handle them well and it will be a creative process. Handle them badly and it will be destructive.'

This is such an important area that this whole third section of the book is devoted to exploring barriers and how to deal with them. In learning to work with barriers successfully we will realise that we can transform the negative energy that is working against us into positive energy that is on our side. In doing so we will also find that the negative names we use can also transform into something else: ally, creative source, supportive friend, exotic muse, unusual quality,

114

internal helper, determination, guts, challenging wisdom.

This kind of transformation is neither magic (though it sometimes feels like it) nor an accident, nor a mystery, but a skill that can be learned and developed.

How to face barriers and deal with them

You have to get to know them. We'll look at how to do that through this section.

How barriers manifest: like groynes...

Let's approach this by using a metaphor to see if we can throw useful light on the subject. I was at the seaside recently, on the East Sussex coast. They have long shingle beaches there. Over the years the authorities who deal with these things have put up groynes, which are like solid timber fences running out from the beach at right angles into the sea. The aim is to prevent beach erosion, to catch some of the shingle as it's transported along the coast by the currents and keep it on the beach.

When the tide is right up you just see the tops of the groynes and the sea and it looks great to swim in. When the tide is out you see not only all the groynes, but the old rotted groynes which have left sharp posts sticking up. If you went swimming without knowing they were there they could bruise or cut your feet and scratch your body painfully.

The barriers within us are like those groynes at high tide. The visible bits of the groynes are the critical voices and the other issues we know about. Submerged just below the surface are the shadowy shapes of the groynes which we start to discern when we swim in the sea. And right at the bottom and only known to us through pain and wounding are the rotted and dangerous ones.

When we do transformative work then it is like lowering the level of the tide – we start to see that which was hidden and can then take remedial action of some kind.

Originally we developed barriers for a useful purpose – usually to protect ourselves when we were little. They may still have a useful purpose, but sometimes they are like rotted relics within us, waiting to catch us unawares, wound us again and again, and make us suffer. And then we sometimes make others suffer too.

What are your barriers?

Which are the ones you know about already and have made progress on?

Which are the ones you know about but they remain in control of you?

Which are the ones you have a little hint of because you get resistant around certain issues?

And finally, which are the ones you have no idea about because they are so deeply buried? Which are your rotted groynes beneath the waves? Those are the real fun ones! If those finally emerge from the depths, they can shape into transformative experiences and transformative poems.

Distraction and other habitual reactions

We'll look at how to handle barriers skilfully in a moment. In the meantime, how might we handle them less well? Handling difficulties poorly may well be one of our habitual patterns. Initially, for example, we might find ourselves looking for distractions rather than solutions. We hope that if we do something else for a while then when we come back it will all be different.

And sometimes, I suppose, maybe it is.

Below are some of the ways I handle barriers poorly. I expect you have your own list that may be similar, or maybe you have your own special elements within it.

So when poems won't come, or I'm stuck, or I'm out of touch with the present moment, or my creativity has dried up, or life gets hard, or God has left me again, or nobody loves me, or whatever... these are the habitual 'poor' responses I revert to:

- I eat
- I watch TV
- I read the newspapers
- I feel very sorry for myself
- I blame a whole bunch of other people
- and things: my past, my nearest and dearest, all those people who did bad things to me, the government, the media, modern life, commercialism, socialism, capitalism, other poets, dumb poets, my teachers at school etc

These are the more 'neutral' responses I sometimes revert to:

- I wash the dishes
- I do work in the garden
- I go for a walk
- I read a 'good' book
- I listen to music

None of these things are 'bad'. As the song says, 'Whatever gets you through the night, it's alright, it's alright.'

117

There is often a value in taking a pause, resting a while, and coming back to the issue refreshed.

To use another analogy, if you're out walking on a snowy mountain path and you've slipped on the path and you're sliding down an icy mountainside out of control, then the first thing to do is to dig in with your ice-axe and bring the slide to a halt. You stabilise the situation, get your breath back, look around and see how you can get back on the path.

The responses we use may be perfectly valid as stabilisers, but become 'poor' if we stick with them too long instead of moving on. Hanging on clinging to an ice-axe for day after day getting more deeply buried in the snow won't do the job.

This next section is all about using skilful means to get back on the poetic path.

Skilful means

We'll look at Critics, Shadows and Eccentricities in turn. In each case we'll see how you can work creatively with these barriers and transform them.

Critics

The critic within is a specific example of a barrier to our expression in our poems, but also in many other aspects of our lives. The critic is the barrier we know about. Here we'll try to concentrate on where the critic is likely to come up in the poem-writing stages, and what we might do about it. Let's keep our eyes open here, people!

Here are some general principles that I'm going to be working within:

- the critic within is a name we give to internalised voices that give critical and negative messages to us
- the messages almost certainly originated in childhood with actual critical messages that we took in and were unable to protect ourselves from
- in adulthood they persist, even when we don't want them to
- they can have a powerful negative and stultifying effect over long periods of time
- it is possible to turn them around but you need to be skilful and persistent
- firstly you have to learn to recognise them and bring them further into awareness; once they are there you can start to work with them
- if you try to suppress them, or ignore them, they will come back
- if you try to fight them they will come back, (though wrestling with them at times may be necessary)
- essentially, you have to welcome them and get to know them; they are part of you, and they are composed of your own energy

- you are aiming to re-incorporate the energy that they represent back into your being in some way
- once the process has started the details will depend on you, your situation, and your creativity. It's a relationship, like any other, except that it starts in enmity. It can grow and develop positively depending on what you do.

Let's pause for a moment here, and reflect. What about you? What do the critical voices inside you say? What are the habitual negative messages that you have to deal with when you are contemplating taking some new action, or shaping up a poem, or putting a piece of your work out into the world? Just take a couple of minutes to reflect upon your own list. Is it long or short? Do you feel familiar with it all, or are there some new elements there? In your life have you managed to sort out your critics or is there still work to do?

Just below here are some of my messages. Yours may be similar, or very different, but whatever they are you will have to work through your own way of handling them, in your own time. But the principles of dealing with them remain the same, as listed above.

So here is an example of an encounter with an internal critic, how I handled it at the time, and how I described it through a poem, this poem:

There is a knocking at my door

There is a knocking at my door.
A determined looking man stands there.
'You have nothing worth saying,' he says.
I try to smile at him, while shrinking a little.
'There may be some truth in that,' I say finally,

'Would you like to come in and talk about it?'

We sit facing each other.
He seems so certain of himself.
'If you do say anything, it will be rubbish.'
'Well,' I say, 'I expect some of my utterings
do come under the heading of clichéd claptrap.
Would you like a cup of tea?'

We sit sipping our tea together.
He seems to come from a different world to me.
'If you do speak,' he says, 'nobody will listen to
 you.'
'You certainly have strong views,' I reply,
and it's a little hard to hear what you say,
'but I appreciate your coming to tell me.'

He gets up to go. 'If they do hear your words,
people will laugh, or be disgusted.'
He seems to speak from bitter experience.
'There's something in what you say,' I reply,
but I guess I have to accept whatever happens.
Sometimes I laugh myself, or feel disgust.'

At the door he pauses.
'You will never come to anything.
Don't even bother trying.
I say this only to protect you from pain.
Do what I say and you will be safe.
There is no-one in the world to trust.'

I reach out gently and try to hug him goodbye.
His body is stiff and unresponsive.
There is hurt held there.

'Thank you for coming', I say,
'I'm grateful for your efforts to look after me,
and I have listened to what you say.'

He heads off down the path.
He seems smaller now, and younger.
I admire his solitary dignity,
and his survival through difficult times.
'Maybe we can work together,' I call,
'See you again tomorrow as usual?'

It's likely that you are familiar with these kinds of messages and have been trying to manage them for most of your life, from adolescence on. You have my sympathy, and my congratulations for your successes so far. I hope that in this next section you can find some confirmation for what you have been doing so far, and maybe some new ideas and support for your future work in this area.

Let's take the messages from the critic in the poem one at a time and tease out some of the implications.

'You have nothing worth saying'

One of the interesting things about this statement is that there is an element of truth to it. Much of what I have in me (and you have in you) is rambling thoughts, or swirling mists of confused words, or shopping lists, or random bits of memory or fantasy. It is not worth saying, and mostly I do not, in fact, say it. It would be a waste of my time and other people's time to say it. Sometimes I do say it, and yes, that just confirms what I should have realised – it wasn't worth the effort of saying it.

But some of what I have in me is worth saying. And sometimes I say it, and sometimes I don't.

When I say it in a poem, I can actually check out whether it was worth saying. I can read it back to myself and feel satisfied that there is truthfulness here that was worth the effort of expressing. And other people can read it and confirm to me that yes, they too, found it of value. Not necessarily everyone, but how many is enough to confirm that there is value here for other people? Ten? Five? One may be enough!

So there is a kernel of truth in what the critical voice is saying, but it is much exaggerated. The critical voice hasn't done the work of sorting out useful truth from a blanket of condemnation.

How do we respond to that kind of criticism – 'you have nothing worth saying'?

In emotional terms we may be upset by it. It sounds like an attack. Maybe it is an attack. Either way we can get into flight or fight mode.

If we are in flight, we try to get away from it, but the message may have got inside us and part of us believes it. Maybe the message follows us in our flight. There is no escape.

Or we try to fight the voice. 'That's bullshit,' we perhaps say, 'who are you to say that? You don't know what you are talking about.'

In fact, in pursuing this perfectly common course of action we are in fact saying to the critic pretty well what they said to us: 'What you are saying has no value. You have nothing worth saying.' This is not really that surprising because the critic is an element of us, and will therefore be quite like us, uncomfortable though that realisation may be.

So the skilful course of action is to get past our tendency for immediate emotional reaction, and try to acknowledge the element of truth within the statement. We are not accepting the truth of the statement as a whole, only a part of it. In doing this we have the basis

123

for a relationship with the voice, and a chance to sort something out that is a more lasting and useful solution to the problem of the critical voice.

In the poem this is expressed like this:

'You have nothing worth saying,' he says.
I try to smile at him, while shrinking a little.
'There may be some truth in that,' I say finally,
'Would you like to come in and talk about it?'

'If you do say anything it will be rubbish'

We can practise the same kind of treatment with this criticism as with the first. How can we acknowledge the element of truth within it, while not giving in to the condemnatory and disempowering intent of the way it is framed?

We can for example, simply acknowledge that it is true sometimes, but not always. Who amongst us does not talk claptrap at times?

But we could also for example change the final word to one that is related to 'rubbish', and find an interesting truth from the phrase as a whole. 'If you do say anything, it will be inadequate.'

If we imagine this being said in a sorrowful, compassionate tone, then the meaning changes considerably, and we can see that it's true in a big way. All that we say in words is inadequate to the reality of what we experience. That's how it is. That is the distressing regime that we exist within when we try to write as poets. The words are always inadequate, but that does not make them 'rubbish.' In fact if we continue to try to point to the glory of what is, with the awareness of our inadequacy always alongside us, then it makes our words into badges of honour, brave attempts to serve a greater purpose when we know, from the beginning, that we will fail.

'If you do speak, nobody will listen to you'

This is also partially true. We could say, if we wanted to respond, that yes, when you write something that matters to you, and which, perhaps, you are confident even expresses some worthwhile truth, there is absolutely no guarantee that anyone will read it. That's how the world works. We have influence but no control.

If we put our poem out into the world, it may or may not be read.

However, there are only two ways to completely guarantee that nobody will listen to what you say, that nobody will read your poem. One, don't write it. And two, if you do write it, keep it secret forever.

If we put our poem out into the world, it may not be read. And a response to that possibility could be, 'Oh well, it's not worth the risk. I won't bother.' A different response could be, 'Hmm. Better make sure I write loads and loads of poems and put them out into the world with as much skill as I can. That will increase the chances of some of them at least being read. And appreciated.'

We all have that choice.

'If they do hear your words, people will laugh or be disgusted'

Well, yes. It's possible, of course.

If we want to engage with our critic here we could respond like this:

'People may laugh or be disgusted, but that's not certain. They may instead be happy, or inspired, or touched, or reminded of their sadness, which is dear to them. They may be amazed, or feel they understand something afresh.

'When you say they will laugh I think that's possibly your fear or bitter experience speaking, which can make us have a distorted view of reality. You have to allow for a whole range of responses when you put out a poem that is part of your being.

'And even if people do laugh or feel disgust, is that so bad? Maybe that is exactly right for them. They need shaking up a bit and this might be the right way to do it. In the end they may be grateful for the shaking up.

'We cannot control how people will respond. And in a way you are right. If we want to make certain that we will never hear laughter or disgust in response to our poems, then we must either not write them, or, having written them, never put them out. It's a choice.'

'You will never come to anything'

Here's a possible response: 'How do you know? You cannot know that. No-one can foretell the future in that kind of way!

'And the only way to find out is to try! So you are incorrect when you say 'Don't bother even trying.' If I follow your advice, then that will make sure that your statement becomes true. But it is not true to start with. You are incorrect here.'

The motivation of the critic is starting to emerge here. As we engage more with them (rather than fight, flight, or ignore/suppress) it turns out that they are not simply out to give us a hard time and malevolently wreck our potential. They are trying to protect us! 'I say this only to protect you from pain. Do what I say and you will be safe.'

If this aspect of the truth emerges from the encounter then we will automatically begin to soften. We understand why they are doing what they are doing. As we soften, so do they (they are part of us). The relationship is on a different footing. We can start to work together perhaps, though depending on the length and depth of the critical voice, it may take some time and involve going over old ground many times.

> He heads off down the path.
> He seems smaller now, and younger.
> I admire his solitary dignity,
> and his survival through difficult times.
> 'Maybe we can work together,' I call,
> 'See you again tomorrow as usual?'

Quick fixes

The strategy for dealing with critical voices, while not wholly accepting, believing, or giving in to what they say, is to welcome them, engage with them, be curious and interested in them, find the kernel of truth within what they say, and see what can usefully emerge from this renewed relationship. This is a long-term aim.

What about short-term tactics, for when we're in the middle of our poem-shaping practice, and those voices start crying, 'Nay! nay! nay! It'll never work!'

Here are some quick fixes I use. They serve the purpose of getting me through the tricky bit, stopping me from giving up, and enabling me to get to the next, more energised, phase. Use these, or create something similar that works for you.

This is not a poem.
Well, maybe not. I'll just write it down anyway and we'll see what happens.

This is going to be no good.
I'm just going to write something down anyway and we can see what it's like later.

This is much too personal/embarrassing/revealing to write about.

You might be right. I'll write it down now, but I won't show it to anyone till later, when I've thought about it.

You've got nothing worthwhile here have you? Give it a miss today.

I'll wait a few more minutes, you never know what's going to show up.

Or: Oh I don't know, there's been a lot happening, but it hasn't had time to come together yet.

There's nothing here is there? Just move along there, nothing to see.

Actually, long experience tells me that you are usually wrong about that. There's plenty here, and some important stuff to see.

Or: actually, for the moment, I'm just going to ignore you.

Or: actually I'm going to prove you wrong. We're not moving from here till I'm ready/I've written a poem/20 more minutes have passed/ my inner Buddha tells me to.

You haven't got time at the moment. Don't bother.

You can sometimes do a lot even in five minutes. I'll do it for a short time anyway.

Shadows

Let's remind ourselves of what we said earlier about shadows:

When we feel a certain kind of resistance to writing poems, or a reluctance to do so, or a blockage, then the likelihood is that we are dealing with shadows. If we feel uncomfortable around certain topics and don't want to look at them in depth, don't want to write poems about them, or just can't get near them somehow, then we are probably dealing with shadow material. We know dimly that something is wrong, or not working, but we can't articulate it, or explain it. We probably feel confusion around it. Nothing quite makes sense, and yet we can't get past it.

For various reasons usually to do with childhood experiences, we have pushed the difficulties below the surface. They remain there out of sight, but affecting us. We do know something is wrong, but we don't know what it is.

The first step to take in handling shadow material is to start to bring it out into the open. Until that happens, we can't work with it.

Blocked

An example of this kind of resistance or reluctance is when you feel blocked.

When you are blocked poetically, then the blockage itself has to become the subject of your enquiry and your potential next poem.

Everything else is a distraction and a deviation from this reality.

At some point you have to stop pushing that which is troubling you back under the surface and, instead, bring it out on to the surface, face it, and deal with it.

The reason you will not want to face it and deal with it is because it will almost certainly involve some degree of discomfort, pain, and suffering.

The bigger the blockage, the less you will want to do it, and the more important it is to do it.

It may take time to come to this realisation. It may take time to find the courage to do it. It may take a long time to work through the issues. But that is the edge where your deepest poetic expressions will come from.

This may be an inconvenient truth, but there is no avoiding dealing with the suffering and discomfort within you if you want to write from your deepest places.

Our instincts are usually to head for the armchair of comfort – who in their right minds heads towards suffering? But to gather yourself into the warmth and comfort of your armchair and cover yourself with a duvet and stay there is to commit poetic suicide slowly. Your poetry, and the poet inside, will die.

This is not, repeat not, saying that all your poetry has to be about your suffering. It is saying that when the door before you is one of suffering and pain then that is what you have to go through. On the other side of that door, hard though it is to believe when you are hesitating before it, is almost always a new and open territory for you to explore and inhabit. This new territory will include joys and passion and delight and insights that were not accessible to you before. These are then your potential poetic subjects until the next blockage or troublesome doorway appears (and it will).

You can choose not to go through that doorway, not to deal with the wounding and suffering that it represents. That is a valid choice. But it comes at a price, and the price is a slow stagnation of your being, your talent, and your poetic expression.

Welcoming the unwelcome

The basic move in dealing with shadows is welcoming them. You have to welcome that which you find unwelcome.

Here's an example. Let us suppose that you are meditating, sitting in the peaceful sunshine, in a clearer space than usual, opening to your deeper self. You have the notion of a poem that may be starting to shape up in you around your joy in nature, and the way that the birdsong you can hear right now connects you with people throughout human existence, all our ancestors.

Then something mildly disturbing crops up in your mind. You ignore it and focus on the birdsong. Then the disturbance comes back, stronger. You find yourself in the midst, say, of a dream from last night where you had to escort a bride to her wedding but she just sat there at the table and didn't seem to want to go and you feel as though you're letting everybody down if you fail to get her there.

You push the dream away and try to concentrate on … what? What was it you were contemplating before the disturbance? Ah yes, birdsong, nature, ancestors.

But it's gone. At this point you realise all that other stuff has gone. You may perhaps be able to return to it another time (though it can never be exactly the same).

The 'disturbance' has now taken over and has become the focus of your work, and of your being, and therefore, potentially, of your poem.

It's hard to make this kind of transition. We want to hold on to the familiar, and what we control. We don't like things just cropping up and then taking over. We may resist it for quite a while.

At some point you have to welcome it. Not just tolerate it, or give in to it, but actively welcome it. You take that which is disturbing you and smile at it. You open yourself to it.

131

If and when you can do that then you can start to work with it.

You can take that which is disturbing you, that which doesn't make sense, and, if you are persistent and fortunate, turn it into something that has meaning for you, and energy for you, and meaning for others.

The story of a transformation can make an extraordinarily good theme for a poem because people love to find out how others deal with difficulties, and how they might be able to do so too.

An example of welcoming the unwelcome

So let's take the wedding dream as an example. If it were me, I would welcome the dream. I might do this either overtly: 'hi dream, I wasn't very keen on you at first, but now I'm happy to meet you and get to know you much better.' Or I might do it simply by the relaxed way in which I start to hold and examine the dream. I might feel this in my body and mind as a warm curiosity, an invitation to the dream to enter the abode of my being, just as if it were an unknown and unexpected guest arriving at my home, in a culture where we welcome guests.

I sit with it and go through the details that I can remember. She's sitting there in her bridal gown and veil at a table in a room, but has no interest in speaking or moving, even though I think they are waiting for her now. I slip off to see what's happening at the wedding. This is not at a church but at a small football stadium, and seems to be scheduled to happen at half-time or after the game. The groom and other guests are happily otherwise engaged in watching the game. I'm on my way back to the bride when I meet someone walking with a horse and cart and stop to talk.

Welcome the disturbance! Welcome the dream, welcome whatever feelings and thoughts start to arise, especially if I'm uneasy about them, if they are unwelcome to me.

What happens if I do that? I make some connections. A couple of days ago my wife and I visited a church set up for a wedding later that day. We thought about the young couple about to set off on their life together. We've also recently had conversations about our youth and I had some regrets about not meeting each other when we were innocent and seventeen.

My thoughts move on. What if I'm the bride here? An insight comes up about this book, which I've just started to write. I'm starting to realise that this is a major project and I will be wedded to my computer for a few months while I finish it. Hmmm. I'm going to have to think some more about that.

I get a buzz out of starting to recognise a truth that wasn't apparent before. There's more there to work on, but you get the picture. That buzz of insight, of truth, is the starting point for a poem if I want to develop it. It comes from welcoming the unwelcome.

It's a great practice. I recommend it to you.

Fill your poems with the transformation of your unwelcome guests, and the insights of your courageous work.

Deliberately focusing on shadows

I've recommended elsewhere in this book that when you come to selecting a topic to contemplate more deeply that you choose something that has energy for you, something that gets your interest going. This makes it more likely that in the early stages of practising this method you will be able to maintain your concentration on the subject and keep coming back to it. Later on, when your skill level improves then you will probably find it easier to focus on a topic whatever your initial level of interest. You find that your interest in the process, and in whatever arises, is sufficient to help you maintain concentration more easily.

So you can choose something you're drawn to. You can also choose something you're repelled by. That also has energy. That also is interesting. Very interesting.

Here's an exercise which you might like to try sometime when you are ready. Are you ready now, perhaps?

What you do is that you choose, as a topic to meditate upon, something which you are reluctant to face. In other words, choose one of your shadows.

Take a moment now and contemplate that possibility. If you were asked to choose a topic you were reluctant to face, what might it be? What might be on the list?

If you haven't done this kind of thing before then it's important to choose a minor reluctance to practise on. Start small, and get used to what might come up and how you might handle it well. Don't start with the biggest ever trauma in your life.

Even little reluctances can lead into surprising insights and consequent shocks to your sense of who you are, of your identity. Take it easy, and take one step at a time. One of the risks of opening up to shadow material is that you can feel overwhelmed. (One of the risks of not opening up to shadow material is that you fossilise and petrify, so there's no easy way out there I'm afraid. Just in case you were thinking that way.)

If you follow the method as we've discussed in this book, then it can be a helpful framework for you. One reason is because you may see after a short time that you already have enough to write a poem about, and can end this stage of the meditation at this point. In other words, it helps you to emerge from looking at shadow material in good time, before you get overstretched. If there's more, you can, if you choose, go back to it on a subsequent occasion. Another reason it may be helpful is that if you write it up as a poem then it is a way of processing and understanding and containing difficult material that might otherwise float around too freely for you.

This exercise is a skilful way of handling barriers, resistance, and shadow. It works because you are taking the initiative to approach the topic rather than wait till it comes to get you. That immediately puts much more of the control in your hands. The balance of power between you and the resistance has tipped in your direction. It hasn't resolved the resistance, but it has made resolution more likely.

Because you have made the choice to enter into this relationship at this point, it also means you have a greater sense of your capacity to exit the relationship when you choose. This is an improvement on the previous situation, where you are expending a lot of energy all the time to keep the shadow under wraps. Sometimes it breaks through against your will and your best efforts. If that happens you're struggling, because you've already been doing your utmost. What on earth are you going to do now?

It takes courage to deliberately sit with and contemplate something you don't want to. But if you can do it, and untie the energy that's bound up there, and let it flow into your writing, you may find yourself doing it, surprisingly, again and again.

The golden shadow

Not all shadow material that we push away from ourselves and bury to one degree or another is 'negative'. It's all 'negative' in the sense that we don't like it – that's why we push it away. But there are two kinds of negative.

Bear with me on this next sentence:

Some of it is negative 'negative', and some is positive 'negative'.

The negative 'negative' is material we don't like because it portrays us in what we consider a 'bad' light to others – we're an angry person, or a jealous one, or a lecherous person.

The positive 'negative' is material we don't like because it portrays us in a 'good' light to others, and we can't yet accept it in ourselves. We don't accept how much we shine. We don't recognise the extent of our talents and abilities. We refuse to see ourselves as the amazing human beings we can be. We push all that away from us, and insist on our smallness and ordinariness.

It is well-named as our 'golden shadow.'

The process for handling our golden shadow is the same as for the 'dark' shadow (welcoming, dialogue, recognition) but the answers may surprise us even more. And tolerating the consequent changes to our self-identity may be even more taxing.

Eccentricities

Let's remind ourselves of what we said earlier about Eccentricities:

Sometimes difficult stuff is so deeply buried within us that we don't have any idea it's there. As far as we are concerned we are completely normal, regular people. It's those guys over there who are the weirdoes.

The main problem with eccentricities, with stuff that is so deeply buried that we don't know it's there... is that we don't know it's there. If we don't know it's there we can't start to bring it out into the open and therefore begin to work with it. It will, unbeknown to us, affect all our relations, including relations with our meditation and our poetry.

There are two main sources of clues about the existence of eccentricities and they both involve other people.

When we see things in other people that we find difficult, or bring up strong feelings in us, then that could be a clue about material hidden in ourselves.

And other people, if they are relatively clear, can see things in us that we can't see in ourselves. If we're able to trust them, then we might learn from them.

Other names for what I'm calling eccentricities, (in an effort to be kind and relatively positive) might include weirdnesses, kinks, neuroses, trouble, difficulties, obsessions.

3-2-1

The basic practice in dealing with Eccentricities is called 3-2-1. It's very effective as a means of accessing inaccessible areas in a way that can translate into satisfying poems. Insight, transformation and healing always carry a wonderful energy with them which communicates really well if you can harness it.

The assumption here is that if we have areas we're in denial about we will get into difficulty of one kind or another. Technical terms here are projection (where we put our unpleasant denied feelings about ourselves out on to someone else) and transference (where we put our unpleasant denied feelings about X out on to Y; classically, for example, we transfer them from our father or mother to the therapist).

The process of correcting this unreal imbalance is one of moving through three stages: seeing the difficulty at first as a third person 'it' (or he or she or they), which is out there somewhere. Then secondly entering into a more direct relationship or dialogue with the 'it' so that the 'it' becomes a 'you' (ie we move into the second person). Then through that process of dialogue recognising and accepting that the difficult issue, the 'you' is part of ourselves. 'It' becomes 'you' becomes (part of) 'I', or first person.

The 3-2-1 process was put together in its current form by Ken Wilber and the Integral movement (gratitude to them). But it has its roots in Gestalt therapy and no doubt other roots further back still.

We can use this process when we suspect that we might be dealing with an Eccentricity. Perhaps we are meditating and an image of someone we dislike comes up, along with associated strong feelings – anger, or contempt, or scorn. We could move into the 3-2-1 process on the assumption that we are dealing with something which is in ourselves, but hidden from us in its details. Perhaps the person has recently done something we don't like. That would make a good place to start.

We can also practice with the 3-2-1 process when we already know that there is something about ourselves which we are reluctant to face. That is, we are more in the area of Shadows than of pure Eccentricity. As mentioned before, the boundaries are not necessarily going to be clear cut. This applies particularly if we have already done some transformation work and started to shift issues from complete unknowns, to dimly unknowns.

If you are new to the 3-2-1 process, it also makes sense to start practicing with an issue you have some knowledge of already. Start learning to surf on little waves before you take your technique and try it out with the big breakers.

Petrified: 3-2-1 in practice

So, in order to make it clearer, here's an example of how 3-2-1 worked in practice, and the poem that resulted from it. The poem describes that process.

The context is that I am contemplating a part of me that I know a little about but am reluctant to face. When I get upset I can become stubborn and cut-off and difficult. It has been so over many years and certainly stems from my childhood. When I'm in that space I'm too upset to do anything but be upset. When I'm not in that space then I don't want to return to it, so it remains mostly untouched, till it comes up again.

On this particular day I'm in a place where I can look at the situation, the energy, without being totally caught up in it. The first thing I do is look at it from the outside, because that's easiest. The difficult figure is over there. It's an 'it', a 'he'. He's in third person. I therefore describe him from the outside.

(Just to be clear, while I'll use the words of the poem that resulted from the experience to help us look at the stages of the 3-2-1 process, the poem emerged from the process, and while it captures that process as best I can, it's not the same.)

Here's that third person stage:

He's sour and bitter enough to set your teeth on edge.
He's a stone-walling, dead-batting lump.
He's a human in the shape of a big, heavy 'NO!'

Well, there's a lot of energy in that lump! He's a powerful figure, even though his whole purpose is to be a nothing, not to engage, to thwart all connection. But the powerful figure is over there, somewhere else, and definitely not me. I'm not that difficult figure. We're separate! We're different! He's somebody else, and he's a bit horrid. Definitely not me.

The 3-2-1 process says that the next move is to try to engage the figure into a relationship of some kind, no matter how tentative. We're trying to get a dialogue going, and the chances are that will be tricky. Usually that is an initiative that you have to take. However here, in this poem, or encounter, the figure takes the initiative:

I hear him telling me to get lost.
'Fuck you' he says. 'Nobody tells me what to do.
I hate you all. I'm scorned and bullied and forced.
I'm damned if I do, and damned if I don't.'

Notice that at this stage of the encounter, the figure is still described in third person mode: 'I hear him telling...' The figure is speaking to me, but I'm just hearing him, not yet engaging with him. He's still a 'he' not a 'you'.

But the figure himself is already in dialogue, in second person ('Fuck you... I hate you all...').

There's a lot of suffering being expressed at this point, ('I'm scorned and bullied and forced') but in a very angry, aggressive way. This is pretty common with suffering that's been untended and ignored for a long time. It goes bad, it turns sour.

How will the encounter proceed? Will it get fully into second person mode? How do I respond? At first, I respond not very skilfully, but I do at least try to engage:

It's hard not to be impatient and angry with him
but that only makes him worse.

So the poem tells us I have responded directly. We're in second person mode. But apparently I've been impatient and irritated with him, and, not surprisingly, he doesn't like it. When we are suffering, it's very easy for an unskilful reaction to make things worse, to increase the anger and the suffering. And on the other hand, anger breeds anger, it sucks us into the fray. It's hard to respond to anger in a non-angry way. I have a go:

Summoning every ounce of compassion I ask him
lovingly to tell me what it's like for him.

This is the crucial turning point in the encounter. I am fully into proper second person mode. I have shown him that I am willing to listen, to really listen, to him. I am willing to be with him, just as he is. I am willing to be engaged with him. How will he respond?

'I have such beauty in me,' he says wistfully.

141

'I'm sad and hurt.
I have such a thick shell.
I can make myself all shell.
All my beauty turns to thick shell.'

He in turn changes. His tone is completely different. Now he doesn't have to defend himself angrily. Instead he can express the sadness that lies behind the anger and the cut-offness. All that beauty turned into a defensive shell – no wonder there is a lot of sadness.

The 3-2-1 process recommends that we try and bring the energy of the 2nd person dialogue into the first person. That we try to integrate what has been manifesting as 'you' into 'I'. How will that work here? What does the poem say happened next?

I am in him and he is in me.
I am scars. I am shell.
I am beauty turning to stone.
I am petrifying beauty.

I take on his message. I recognise that as it is with him, so it is with me. I too am scars and shell. I too have turned my beauty into shell, into stone.

As I write this paragraph about the poem, I am again filled with the sadness of all this – not only sadness at my own loss, but sadness at all the beauty in all the people of the world who for reasons beyond their control have learned to turn their beauty into hard shells.

When energy shifts as a result of a process like 3-2-1 then it shifts, and what was held will become fluid again. As with all feelings, you feel it! It is not an intellectual exercise. Be prepared for the unknown, and let that, if you can, flow through into your poetry.

The encounter has not quite finished. I am looking for wisdom from this. I am looking for a solution to the shell problem. I turn to my figure again, but this time for help. Notice how he has now changed from an enemy to an ally. I trust him now. I actively want his input.

Here's the whole poem for you to read and find out what he said.

Petrifying beauty

He's sour and bitter enough to set your teeth on
 edge.
He's a stone-walling, dead-batting lump.
He's a human in the shape of a big, heavy 'NO!'

I hear him telling me to get lost.
'Fuck you' he says. 'Nobody tells me what to do.
I hate you all. I'm scorned and bullied and forced.
I'm damned if I do, and damned if I don't.'

It's hard not to be impatient and angry with him
but that only makes him worse.
Summoning every ounce of compassion I ask him
lovingly to tell me what it's like for him.

'I have such beauty in me,' he says wistfully.
'I'm sad and hurt.
I have such a thick shell.
I can make myself all shell.
All my beauty turns to thick shell.'

I am in him and he is in me.

I am scars. I am shell.
I am beauty turning to stone.
I am petrifying beauty.

'What next?' I ask him.
'It's only love,' he says, 'will turn it round.'

What about you? Is there some tricky issue in your life at the moment? Is it 'over there' somewhere? What about closing your eyes right now and seeing it. Then entering into some kind of dialogue, then seeing if you can bring (some of) it closer to home, perhaps right back home.

Maybe later there's a poem that reports what happens for you.

Section 4. Moving on to a different level

The book so far has given you have everything you need to go, go, go with your shaping of poems from deeper in your being. But as you go on, then some other questions are going to come up for you - of course. Here are my attempts to predict some of those questions and provide you with some clues as to how to handle them.

So who are you writing for?

This question relates to 'Intention' which is about giving yourself a clear focus to help you sit in meditation and wait for greater clarity to manifest. Your 'intention' is an answer to the question, 'What will I do with the next hour or so of my life?'

'Who are you writing for?' poses a different question which will have a longer-term impact on how you shape poems, how you edit them, which subjects you choose, what you feel you cannot say, what you feel you can say, and other issues.

As ever in this book, I'm going to recommend awareness (mindfulness) as the important guideline. Conscious awareness. Why is that important? Because if you are not consciously aware of who you are writing for, then you will be unconsciously writing for someone. And that someone will probably cause problems.

Take a few moments right now, close your eyes, and ask yourself two questions. 'Who would I love to write for?' 'Who would I be really worried about writing for?'

Get any answers?

Another way to frame these questions would be, 'If I imagine someone reading my poems, who can I imagine who would love and appreciate them, and who could I imagine being critical and sour?'

Now if and when our poems go out into the world then there may indeed be people who read them who are critical or dismissive or sour or contemptuous or rude or disapproving or condescending or...

And if that happens then we will have to handle that at that time. (Hey, at least they've read the poems!) But the key point is that if those kinds of people are unconsciously around in your mind at the time you are shaping or editing your poem, they will influence it. Your writing will be more scared, more defensive, narrower, more conventional and risk-averse.

Another way to say this is that you will design your poems to fit in better with the prejudices of those people who have not got your best interests at heart. Why would you want to do that? Really, why would you?

Well, I hear you say, one answer is to avoid the scarifying kind of pain that I might have experienced previously. And of course that's right.

So what's the answer to this? Let's go back a bit.

'But the key point is that if those kinds of people are unconsciously around in your mind at the time you are shaping or editing your poem, they will influence it.'

Notice that word 'unconsciously'? It's different if you are aware of those figures. Once they are there in your awareness you can manage them. (We've looked in more detail at ways of doing this in the 'Barriers' section of the book.) In the long-term, you have to engage with them. But in the short-term you can simply order them out, for example. Or laugh at them. Or you can use their presence as motivation to go on in ways that would really spite them, that would really piss them off. Sometimes this is just the energy you need to push yourself into a new area you were reluctant to enter.

So what we want to do is create a situation where, when you are shaping a poem, the figures that are with you in your mind (if any) are the kind of figures who will support and believe in you, who will help you keep that creative space open and safe, so that those new things that matter to you can emerge and be born.

Hence the importance of knowing who you are writing for. You choose. You invite them to be present. They haven't just turned up unasked as they may do in other aspects of your life. (If they do, show them the door!)

So contemplate who would be a great figure, or figures, to invite into your life, your mind, your clarity, your poetry. If you do this, then it's important that you make the choice yourself. Sometimes that takes a while to feel into and decide. In the meantime, here are some examples:

- 'There was this one teacher at school. When everyone else took the mickey out of me, he really believed in me, he saw my potential. I write for him.'
- 'I write for my mother. She's dead now but she always loved everything I did. When I think of her reading my stuff, I smile, and I see her smiling.'
- I write for my kids. I love them so much, and I know they love me. They are with me when I write.'
- 'I write for God. He's a really cool dude, and is interested in everything I do. Nothing phases him. He's always looking over my shoulder, joking with me, and supporting me to go on.'

- 'When I write, somewhere at the back of my mind I have this image of Truth. It's like she's a beautiful but enigmatic woman sitting there. She doesn't do anything overtly, but if I'm not right on the truth, I know she knows.'

Sitting in contemplation:
My everyday mind won't go quiet

My everyday mind won't go quiet – all that comes up for me is planning and reviewing and worrying at stuff.

We touched on this before. We identified that the standard response would be to say, just keep persisting; notice the way you are stuck in your everyday mind and then, compassionately and good-humouredly, return to your breathing. And indeed sometimes this is sufficient, and you gradually develop that capacity for quiet where your everyday mind takes a rest.

And I also identified that sometimes stronger measures are necessary: for a deeper understanding and longer-term solution you might have to consider the kind of approach I'll describe next.

First check this out with yourself: am I considering my everyday mind as a 'problem'? Am I perhaps even considering my everyday mind as 'the enemy'? If you are (and it would be perfectly common to do so) then you are setting up a conflict between your 'self' and your 'everyday mind.' This will absorb a lot of energy, leave both sides exhausted and probably result in an unpleasant stalemate.

It's better, more compassionate to all parties, and most importantly, more effective, to work instead along these lines.

Take great care to regard your everyday mind as a valued and vital part of your being. Because it is! Have a conversation with it in which you express this clearly. For example:

'Everyday mind, I just want to tell you what a great job you do so much of the time. You are so busy running my life, making sure I'm OK and can function in the world, organising my shopping lists and to-do lists, remembering important meetings and planning for them, really looking after me and keeping me safe. I couldn't function without you. I value what you do for me so much, and I want you to know that.'

Now this has to be sincere. You can't fake this kind of stuff, or just repeat my words by rote. You have to mean it. The everyday mind is not a fool – one of its specialities is scepticism. So if you can't say it for real, you need to go away and do some work on it. Look at the issue deeply, and consider what your normal, rational, worrying, everyday mind actually does for you. Clue: a lot!

Now once you've done that you can move on to the next stage.

This is where you ask the everyday mind to take a break. You're saying something like:

'Everyday mind, I'd like you to take a little rest for a short while. You do a great job, but even you need to rest sometimes. I want to get into a different space in my mind and I can only do that while you sit on the sidelines resting.'

Notice that we're being invitational – we're asking, not giving orders. This is not just old-fashioned good manners, but because the everyday mind is used to being in control. If it senses a power struggle with someone else who is trying to take over then it will fight back, and we've got a return to an exhausting conflict.

But the everyday mind is very suspicious. It may be saying to itself, 'Hmmm, they're asking me to take a rest, which sounds reasonable, but what if it's a trick? What if while I'm innocently resting they institute a coup, capture me and lock me up so I can't do my job making sure their life runs properly. No fear! I'm staying alert and in control. I'm keeping going...'

So this is where we try to bring in reassurance. We make sure the everyday mind knows it still has a job to do, and is still valued (which it should be). We say something like:

'I just want you to rest for a short time. You can watch if you like, as long as you stay quiet. And then there will be an important job for you to do. Once I've got past my quiet period of contemplation and written down my poem, there will be decisions to take and that's where you come back into the picture because decision-making is what you are good at.'

After this the rational everyday mind should be happier because it loves making decisions: evidence, thinking, options to consider, decisions to make, power, control, influence...

And indeed this is the case, because once you enter the editing phase, you are mostly utilising the rational part of your mind. And later on there is more 'everyday' processing to do: filing it, sending it out, re-editing it etc. And for those purposes, you really do need your rational, everyday mind to be functioning effectively and well.

Meditating on a topic:
How far can I go from the topic?

When I'm meditating on my topic, as long as I'm aware of what I'm aware of, how far can I go from the topic before I should come back?

I think it depends on the level of clarity that you are operating within. At the super clarity level, you are never off or away from the topic because you know, and see, and realise, in an intimate way, just how everything is connected to everything else. This is not an intellectual understanding, but a moment by moment reality to you. I'm smiling as I write this, because even to know that this is possible is very joyful.

If you are operating at a level of clarity beyond the everyday but not super-clear, then circling around your topic is safer for the purposes we have in mind (insight leading to poetry). I'm thinking here of a process like mind-mapping, where the central topic leads to various connections. You can move from one connection to another while staying close to the central bubble. This would be like holding the topic in one part of your mind while following links nearby. Or you can move from connection to connection in a way that takes you further afield – off the page and on to another, so to speak. The risk here is that if you do lose the thread when you are a long way from 'home' (the original topic) you may lose much of the intervening stuff you've been connecting with.

This is an 'advanced' area, if you like, and one that if you were interested in, you could play around with some more and see what you can learn.

What about making notes?
...during meditating on the topic

I really feel that I can't hold everything in my mind when I'm meditating around my topic. Is there any way I can note things down part way through the process and still be within it?

You can experiment all you wish and find out what works best for you. That is the final criteria of 'success'.

The first reason I've emphasised holding stuff in your mind and writing it down later is to give support to the creative process within you and allow it the time it needs to come to fruition. The tendency in our culture is to rush to production and achievement too quickly for depth to emerge. It takes time to get down deep, especially if you are not familiar with that area. Coming out too soon to take notes will at the least interrupt that process, and at worst bring it to an end.

The second reason I've emphasised holding off writing anything down until it's all there is in the interests of wholeness. The poem comes together as a whole rather than being composed of bits that don't necessarily gel. The risk of writing notes part way through is that the final poem will feel, seem, and be 'bitty' and that some important links and connections that would otherwise have been there will be lost.

However if you are going to experiment with notes here's what I would suggest.

Regard this as a staging post to what you are finally aiming at. So keep stretching yourself to retain material for longer and longer. Don't give yourself the easy way out all the time. Be aware if you find yourself noting things down every few seconds.

Make your note-taking as brief and 'unthinking' as you can. You could take lessons from someone I once read on writing down dreams. They recommended having a note book and pen by your bed in a precise place. You could then half-wake in the night, immediately find the notebook in the dark, and (with practice) be able to scribble down a few words of reminder without putting on the light, and without waking up properly. You are still half in the dream state.

Keep asking yourself also: how much of my conviction that I cannot retain material in my mind is 'real' and how much is anxiety born of habit and pressures in earlier parts of my life? Keep testing. Maybe it's not 'real' and you find you can retain far more than you thought.

Maybe it is 'real' and you do have difficulties. You can still work with the knowledge that this is a skill that you can work on and develop.

Disturbances: ignore? or work with?

It's a common, standard, 'problem' in meditation. There you are, meditating happily away, and a distracting force – for example anger – comes up. What do you do? Classic answer: as little as possible. You become aware of it, and then let it go. You are practising non-attachment: not suppressing, but not getting caught in it either.

Sometimes this works for us, but sometimes it really doesn't! We're curious about ourselves and want to know more. And sometimes parts of us really want to be better known! Those parts keep coming up more and more forcefully. How to handle this?

I like watching 'The Dog Whisperer' on TV. Cesar Milan is a truly extraordinary teacher – of dogs, for sure, but also of people. This example caught my attention. He was instructing someone about how to handle difficult dog behaviour. He threw in this advice, pretty casually: "Imagine the dog behaviour you're trying to correct is on a scale of 1-10. Scale 1-5 you ignore it; scale 5 -10 you gotta deal with it."

Wow! That makes so much sense. If you pay attention to minor stuff the risk is you get caught up in it. If you fail to deal with major stuff the risk is it takes you over.

As with dog, so with meditation.

So try experimenting with this guidance. Minor irritation – notice and let go. Keep focusing on your topic. Big anger and fury: move into an active mode of inner work on the new topic. Stuff in the middle: a judgement call one way or the other.

Nothing in the universe

Here's another exercise I've used with groups. You might like to try it. Mostly in this book when we've been considering topics to focus on in the meditating stage of the method, we've concentrated on internal subjects: the memory of an experience or event, other aspects of our mind, a feeling in the body.

It's also possible to go outside, find something that attracts you for some reason (or repels you...) and sit with that as your topic. What do you notice about the object, and what comes up in you?

Natural objects (trees, plants, hills, streams, leaves, flowers, shadows) often work well.

I have a theory on this (I have a theory on many things...). The theory is this: because we are creatures who have developed through the aeons of our existence in natural surroundings we are peculiarly attuned to them. And because the aeons of our existence as a species were predominantly spent in a pre-verbal stage, then being in tune with natural objects in a natural setting helps us to access the non-verbal stage more readily. For the purposes of writing poetry of this kind, we can bypass our (verbal) everyday mind more easily and connect directly with the experience of the moment.

Usually, from a depth point of view, it's not the tree or leaf, or flower itself that concerns us, but the relation between that flower and our inner life. We notice what comes up in the 'outer' world and what arises in our 'inner' world, and maybe start to realise that the boundaries between those two worlds are not as clear as we once thought.

So, natural objects in a natural setting can be particularly inspiring for some people.

But buildings, or sheds, or cars and motorways, or football matches, also exist in the universe, and are worthy of your intimate attention.

Remember, there is nothing in the universe that you cannot write a poem about. There are no two things in the universe that you cannot connect in some way and write an insightful poem about.

Extra ways to 'go deep' or 'get clear'

Getting access to states of greater clarity is neither a mystery nor an accident, but a matter of skilled practice. And that means you can learn how to do it. In this book I focus on meditation, because my experience says it is particularly well suited to the process of shaping up poetry.

However, other means may work better for you and your poetry, or they may work better for a different kind of creative expression, or they may work really well as an adjunct to your meditation-based poetry writing.

Please notice that 'altered' states of mind (that is, different in kind from everyday states of mind) are not necessarily deeper, clearer states of mind. They may provide a route into clarity, or a supportive framework for getting there, or they may flatter to deceive and just be a dead-end. You have been warned.

Here's a rough guide to a few possibilities. If I don't provide links, then you are just going to have to use your own research methods. (Hint: try Google…)

Experiment with Light is a Quaker practice of what could be described as guided meditation. This was originally developed by Rex Ambler, who wanted to re-connect with the practices of George Fox and the early Quakers that led them to have such deep and powerful connections to the Light (Spirit, the Divine, God). There are local groups that meet, and workshops, and on-line resources. I'm a big fan, and have almost always found it very powerful as a way of accessing that which is normally beyond everyday life. Part of the strength of the practice (as with Quaker worship generally) is that it is collective. You are part of a group and benefit (or sometimes suffer) from that environment.

Big Mind is a modern day offshoot of Zen, developed in the States. It enables you to identify different voices/parts within you, and seek the help and permission of some of them (eg the Controller) in order to access others that are often more hidden. Big Mind (linked to Buddha nature, or natural mind, or Emptiness, or God) would be one of those usually hidden parts. I read the book, and I liked it, and the practice took me to some unusual places.

Prayer. If you have for example, a strong Christian practice, then prayer will be a means through which you may well be familiar with accessing a clearer, deeper state, closer to God. I am thinking here more of the personal intimate relationship with God that you may develop through private prayer, and contemplation, and listening. Father Thomas Keating's Centering Prayer is a supportive, systematic approach to this.

Love. Falling in love is a classic way to experience an altered state. Everything sparkles, huh? Some people get hooked on it in a serial kind of way. There are problems with that...

On a more practical note, most spiritual traditions emphasise love, or gratitude, or compassion, or open-heartedness as ways to practise, both in and for themselves, and as a path to deeper connection with all things. The traditions have accumulated wisdom in these areas over centuries. They are worth taking very seriously.

Dance. In a survey on what brought most joy to people, dance came top of the list. (Volunteering came second.) Dance brings more physical awareness, more awareness of breathing, less emphasis on the rational everyday mind. You can see the links to meditation. Some circle dancing, for example, is very quiet, profound and repetitive. (Some is wild and ecstatic.) Dance is a whole very large subject area in itself, with many different types and flavours. Much to explore, much to enjoy, much to experiment with in terms of accessing deeper, clearer spaces.

Psychotherapy can help you sort out those barriers within you that prevent you from living fully, from opening your heart, from being the person you could be. There are now a lot of varieties to choose from and explore (with more developing every day). Some are more overtly focused on development of inner clarity than others. I don't know them all, but I do like:

POP Process Oriented Psychotherapy which provides you with lots of tools in order to work positively and creatively with whatever is coming up in you, and in your world. The distinctions between 'inner' and 'outer' are not rigid in POP and the work can move rapidly backwards and forwards between them, amongst them, around them...

Drugs. Chemicals can have an impact, but I recommend accessing greater clarity the natural way. There's more on this just below.

You could also consider approaches like: self-hypnosis, visualisation, listening to specialised CDs that take you deep. Music in all its variations is another classic access point for altered states.

Drugs and all that

Poets and writers have used drugs to help them enter altered states. Mystics have sometimes done the same. Shamans in tribal cultures utilise them.

Coleridge used opium. Dylan Thomas used alcohol. The beat generation used marijuana. There are plenty of examples.

It's an option. It's your body, your being, your poetry, your choice.

It depends partly upon your values, partly upon your view of risk, and partly upon practicalities.

It's an interesting area and you can follow up if you want. In this book I take a particular line on this which is based on the practicalities for your poetry not on morality or health risks. I'll take you through it.

We can understand the choices better if we understand the wider context. For these purposes let's define a drug as a chemical substance that has an impact on your state of mind via your body.

At the low level, this includes all the food you eat. Then there's the tea and coffee you drink. If, for example, you drink a lot of strong coffee per day that's actually having quite a powerful impact.

Further up the scale is alcohol. We also hit the (mostly) illegals: marijuana, LSD, magic mushrooms etc. Different drugs, different impacts on your body and mind. Some are mostly depressants, some psychedelics, some relaxants. The interplay between drug, individual, social context, and state of mind is not simple and causal.

Chemicals can and do get you to unusual places. What are the potential downsides?

An analogy that comes to mind is this. Accessing a clearer state of mind is like climbing a mountain. It takes effort, and practice, but when we get up there we know we have had the full experience. Because the experience was also about climbing the mountain, not just getting to the top. And we know the way there; we know it intimately and well. We can get up there again another time because we know the way. We can get back down again, because we know the way. We are confident with our own ability to do so. We acclimatise our body gradually to the different atmosphere up there.

Using a drug to get there is like being helicoptered in. You won't know the way there. Getting to the top suddenly without acclimatisation may be a shock to your system. If you crash-land part way up, you won't necessarily know the way down either.

If you do use drugs to access altered states of mind, there are two major risks (for your poetry that is. Health risks you'll have to consider for yourself.)

One is that you generally come to rely on the drug to access the state. You come to believe that the state is contained within the drug. What happens if the drugs stop working? Suppose you build toleration to the dose for example? What happens if you can't get hold of the drug? We're in the territory of addiction here, and it's sometimes unpleasant. What you've done is ceded your own power and control to a non-responsible chemical substance. Get it back! That's my advice. Get your own power back and keep it.

The second disadvantage is that you start to confuse the drug's (toxic) 'side' effects with your own inner reality. You may feel nauseous and bitter under the influence. You may have visions. Which is God, and which is your bodily reaction to some alien substance?

If you have entered a non-everyday state in a 'natural' way, then you can have more confidence that what you have experienced is truer and more reliable. And anyone who reads your poems can too. When I read a poem that touches on deeper issues, I'm looking for clues as to how authentic this is. Can I trust the writer? To what extent are they the real deal? Have they done the work, or are they faking it?

Drugs, illegal and legal, all act on the sensitivity of your body, mind and being to what is. If you want to be more in touch with what is, then what you need to do is protect yourself from undue influences, and persistently practise being open to what is.

Be aware not only of what you eat, drink, smoke or ingest, but also of what you read, listen to, or watch. Certain films, songs, or writings may also have toxic effects on you, on your being, and on your sensitivity to what is.

Why go deeper?

Because you are designed to do so! Because you get a sense of dissatisfaction if you're not operating at the right level for you. If you're too shallow you won't feel right. You know that, don't you? That's familiar to you, and to your friends.

On the other hand, you don't have to go any deeper than is right for you at this time (it's not a competition with other people; this is your gig, not theirs). You can stay wherever is right for as long as it's right, then you have to move on, whether you want to or not (and often you don't want to). That seems to be the deal.

The relation of inner dialogue to inner depth

What about those times when we hear words and voices inside our minds? Isn't that part of our inner life, our deeper life?

We need to distinguish if we can between two forms of dialogue here. When we first sit down to meditate our minds may well be filled with chatter. That's usually the busyness of the everyday mind. It is possible to work with this, but it would be very challenging, especially if you are a relative beginner at all this. It's better to stay with the getting clear process until you have achieved a relative level of clarity.

Through this process you find, for example, that the chatter has slowed right down and then stopped. You are aware of your breathing and aspects of your body. Maybe the sounds of the day that you usually miss are apparent to you.

When you have some kind of stability in this space then allowing dialogue and voices to arise is of a different order. You have some measure of influence on what is happening. The voices and words you hear do not crowd out all else but take place in a more spacious environment. It's possible for you to observe what's going on rather than be at the mercy of energy that takes you over. You have more choice. If you start to feel crowded out by what's happening you can return to your breathing and re-establish a place of greater clarity.

When you are able, in this place of greater clarity, to observe and also join in dialogue and inner conversations then this can be a rich source of insight that can translate well into poems.

Sometimes those words and conversations are at a 'shallower' level than when we go in really deep; that is, we are still at a conceptual level. There's nothing wrong with this. We know what's happening, we enjoy it and work with it.

And sometimes those words and conversations are themselves verbal translations of the forces that are swirling in us beyond our words. That is, our mind has already done some of that translation job for us from the non-conceptual to the conceptual.

What about creating a list of topics outside meditation?

I'm in favour of experimenting and finding out what works for you. Try it and see, but expect your habits and preferred methods to change over time.

I've kept a small notebook in which I briefly note topics that interest me, or affect me, or that have occurred to me with some kind of energy that says, 'Come back to this and look at it more deeply sometime.'

Sometimes I do, sometimes I don't. Sometimes I look at the subject and there's no longer a buzz, or a connection. Sometimes I've addressed it already but from a different point of view.

I also have periods when I don't keep a notebook of topics, and simply rely on whatever arises in the moment when I'm sitting. Sometimes it's very simple, sometimes difficult. Sometimes nothing arises – or nothing that I'm in a state to pursue from a poetic point of view.

If what we are trying to do is access that which is more real, that which exists in this moment as real, that which is currently unknown in some way, then we have to accept whatever occurs. We can influence but not control what happens.

At one time I experimented in this way, so this is potentially something else to try. As I first sat in contemplation I would have a notebook handy. As my mind began to settle, I would notice the thoughts or images that came up. As each occurred I would make a very brief note in the notebook, naming it. As the list grew, it would often become apparent which topic had a draw for me, and so I would then focus on that.

The advantage of doing it this way is that there is a discipline in attending to what is arising which helps prevent getting lost in the thoughts. It's a variation on a standard meditation practice of 'naming' the thoughts as they arise, but which is usually done silently and in one's mind. The disadvantage of doing it this way is that it interrupts the process of 'settling down' and gradually entering a clearer space.

What is truthfulness?

When we talk about truth in the context of the poetic method in this book (how truthful is my poem?), the aspect of truth we are dealing with here is what Ken Wilber calls truthfulness (as opposed to some more objective, outer truth).

Nobody can see into our minds and therefore they cannot measure and argue about the truth of something from inside us in the same way as they can about something outside that we can all see (the football score, or who was at the party last week).

Truthfulness therefore rests with you, the poet, and how you decide to manifest it, and how consistently you do that. From outside, we the readers have to decide how much we will trust the poet's truthful expression of their experience.

Poetry: a distraction from my pilgrimage?

In classical meditation terms, anything that takes you away from your focus on awareness of this moment, or the nature of mind, or emptiness, would be seen as a distraction. Whatever it is – bliss, suffering, joy – your practice is to be aware of it coming up, aware of it hanging around a while, and then aware as it passes. You don't hold on, or engage.

So yes, being interested in shaping poems from this perspective could well be a distraction from that process. More poems might equal less spiritual progress on your journey.

On the other hand, it's your journey. You have to make it on your terms. Otherwise it's somebody else's journey and that won't work for you.

We can think of it as a pilgrimage. There are well-travelled routes. There are people to make the pilgrimage with. But the journey throws up its own choices: a route along the back ways rather than the highway; a detour to see a particular shrine; an attraction to a small group that is travelling more slowly.

Maybe you get tired and you need to rest for a few weeks or months or years at a particular place that attracts you. Maybe you realise this place is in fact your destination and you are not going to journey any further; or more accurately, that your journeying will take a different form from here on. Maybe you can go home now, or maybe you realise that you are already home.

So poems may be a distraction from your journey, or they may be a support for your journey, or they may be your journey itself. How do you tell? Stay aware through the uncertainty, informed by your meditational insights, your dreams, the urgency of your sense of mission, and guidance from teachers and traditions that have been through this before.

There are poems and then there are poems. The ecstatic insights of Rumi are only remotely connected to the verse in a contemporary literary magazine. I doubt Rumi thought of poetry in the same way that we do. But there's no reason why we can't think of poetry more like he did.

Doesn't this book complicate things?

You said somewhere that you thought it was easy to make simple things complicated and harder to make complicated things simple. Isn't this whole book just a complication of something very simple?

Hmmm. Yes at heart, the poem-shaping process is very simple: you sit with a topic and meditate upon it, let words form around it, shape them into a poem and write it down. Pretty simple. In fact I say at the beginning of the book that you don't actually need the book, you can just do it. Just doing it is what I did. You can do the same – and maybe arrive at a different method.

I'd say that the book is not complicated, but detailed, and that's different.

Let's use the analogy of exploring unknown territory. You can just walk into that territory, mapless, and explore it. You can wander around in it, get lost in it, and eventually wander out again (or stay lost...). You can keep going back in and eventually feel you've got to know it. You have a rough map in your head, and maybe some sketches you share with other people.

So I'd invite you to regard this book as a detailed map of a particular territory (writing poems from a deeper place of meditation). You don't actually need a map, but it may make your exploration a lot easier if you have one. You can use it to go further than I did, without having to learn all the stuff I had to from scratch. You can eventually draw up a better map. One day someone will.

What if the subject feels too big?

Maybe you've had a powerful experience of love, or connection to the divine, or to nature. You know it's important, and you'd love to write about it, but you don't feel worthy, you don't feel adequate to the task. How can you possibly do it justice? How can your words point accurately to the experience and communicate the depth of connection you felt, and the importance of the insights you were granted?

It's a problem. Sometimes it is important to delay attempts to write about something until you and the experience have matured and are ready. This might be a few days, but it might be months, or years.

In the meantime you could simply meditate upon the experience, enjoy it, and keep looking at it deeply. This will help to keep it fresh within you, and support that maturation process.

Maybe you could write something anyway, but tell yourself it's not the final version, only like a preparatory sketch before the real painting. Maybe that will be the case, but maybe your sketch turns out to be the real thing, as good as you're going to get.

Sometimes telling yourself you need to wait is a way of avoiding doing what you need to do right now.

You may be afraid you are not adequate, but do it anyway, despite the fear. That sounds like bravery!

How can you tell when delay is needed and right, and when delay is fear and procrastination? I suspect if I could give a succinct answer to that question my fortune might be made. Perhaps one clue would be in your attitude to the future writing process. If you find yourself looking forward to being able to tackle the subject when you have a little more perspective and wisdom about it, it sounds like it's OK to wait. Otherwise, make a start right now, and see how it goes. You may be surprised.

The ethical dimension to writing poems

We know from the 'barriers' section of the book that we have hidden material within us (the difficult stuff we don't want to face, the difficult stuff we are only dimly aware of, or not aware of at all). If we don't deal with this material then it will find its way into our poems unbeknownst to us. It will just seem like normal stuff.

Now to my mind this creates a problem. How big a problem it is for you depends on your values, and your ethical stance.

Suppose someone has an unresolved issue around violence and cruelty. Perhaps awful things happened to them as a child and they've dealt with the problem by burying it. As a child you don't have much choice. You have to do whatever gets you through it. Later, as an adult those buried feelings may (may, not will) manifest as a fascination with cruelty and pain. If that fascination is unprocessed, unworked on, unfaced, it will find its way into whatever poetry that person writes. It may then be accepted by others as 'art' or 'literature'.

That doesn't fit with my sense of what a good human being does. As the Buddha said: 'My work is suffering, and the transformation of suffering,' and it's that second part that I'm interested in here. I'm compassionate and patient with those who are suffering and who want help to transform their

167

suffering. I'm much less patient with those who just spread their suffering around. There's no need. We know too many ways to work at transforming that suffering. We need to stop ourselves spreading more suffering, and we need to stop others doing it. This applies just as much to poetry as anywhere else.

There's another way of saying that.

I'm now going to indulge myself in a short rant. If you don't like short rants please skip the next few lines. This is aimed at ignorant and selfish poets, and the ignorant and selfish poet within me:

"If you think it's OK to spread your unprocessed weirdness all over other people's consciousnesses, then think again. It's bloody not OK. Be responsible. Be ethical. Do the work!"

Can critics be useful?

For sure. I value some of my inner critics in this way. I sometimes find myself caught up in imagining what 'outer critics' will say about my work when it appears in the world. At some point I like to consider what they say (or what real critics out there might say...), especially if it's negative, which it often is. This is also the method I try to use with actual (not inner) negative criticism that comes my way.

My question is: how much truth is there in what they say? I try to consider this seriously. Some part of what they say might, in my eyes, be correct. If that is so, then thanks, critics, I'm going to make some changes here and improve my work before it gets out there in the world. I want to make it as good as I can. I don't want errors or imprecision left in to haunt me. I'm willing and eager to test out my work before it hits a wider audience.

If it's not correct, then I can just leave it. It's some problem of theirs that they are going to have to sort out. Sometimes I take my chance at this point to have a go at them and really assert my own truth and approach in the matter. They're only internal critics, they can take it!

If I think they're wrong, but I'm upset by the criticism, then the likelihood is that it is true in some way but I won't accept it. I need therefore to do some work there and find out more.

How much other poetry should I be reading?

Not too many 'shoulds' in this book! And hopefully not too many in your life. Remember there's poetry and poetry. There are people, including possibly people who love you, who have strong views on what poetry they like, and don't like, and maybe what will be good for you. Ultimately, none of this matters very much. What matters is what gives you energy to go on and live and love and be alive as fully as you can.

Here's a definition of good music that I came across thirty years ago: 'Good music is music that raises the level of life energy in you.'

Here's a variation on that for this question: 'If poetry doesn't make you breathe more easily, touch your emotions, and make you feel more deeply connected, don't read it.' You get the picture. I suggest you make up your own version of that.

Remember there's poetry and poetry. Going back to a music analogy, it's likely that if you are interested in writing folk-songs you might listen to other folk-songs, but there would be less value in hip-hop. (OK, you might want to write folk song that has hip-hop influences, but you know what I mean).

If you want to express your joy and devotion to God through writing hymns, then heavy metal might not be particularly helpful.

I'd suggest you choose any poems you read on the same basis, recognising that there are in poetry widely different categories, as in music, but, for some reason, less well labelled.

And don't necessarily believe the labels. I've seen poems labelled 'spiritual' that left me cold. In my definition, they weren't.

And really, don't feel under any obligation to read anything. You are on your journey, doing it in your way. At some point you may well need to leave off being influenced by what other people say they experience, and concentrate on expressing and communicating your unique perspective on it.

Personally I have found it almost impossible to read any poetry over the last five years that isn't 'from deep' in the way I describe in this book. This is the period during which I have been focusing in a disciplined way on shaping poems from a space of meditation. Impossible. I don't mean, 'I don't like to' or 'prefer not to' or 'I'm just too busy.' I mean that whenever I try to read it I feel physically nauseous and can't go on. Hmmm. That's the way it is. It's a bit tricky when people try to recommend to me some interesting poems they want me to look at, but that's the way it is.

I talked to a sculptor recently and he told me that when he's working on a piece he can't look at other sculptors' work. When it's finished he then goes round wolfing down what's been happening while he's been caught in his creative space.

What makes poetry alive?

When it comes from the growing edge of the poet. When the poet is wrestling with issues that matter to them. When the poet is communicating the new and the fresh, and that which is of this moment.

What makes poetry dead? When it's been said before in the same way. When the poet is bored with it all. When the poet is treading water, going over familiar territory, writing for someone they don't respect and love.

What makes poetry false? When the poet is claiming an authority they don't have. When they haven't done the work on themselves. When they are writing for kudos, or fame, and to fit in with what's required by their poetry community. When they are not being true to themselves because they don't know what their truth is, or they know what it is but have settled for something less, a comfortable poetic life.

Conclusion

This book is nearly over! I've taken you through 'the Method' in a variety of ways, and in a lot of detail. We've looked also at the Barriers that can prevent you from expressing yourself and communicating through poetry (or any other way); and we've looked at some of the powerful ways you can transform those barriers. And in the last section we looked at various questions that arise as you become more experienced at shaping up poems from a deeper place, and the ways in which you can move forward.

In this conclusion I just have a few more important points to make, some encouragement to offer, and some skilful means to share, and then it really is over to you. What will be your next step...?

Two advantages we have these days

We actually have two main advantages over traditional poets if we want to pursue our poetic explorations. I'm not talking about the internet, or computers, or Amazon self-publishing here, although they are pretty helpful.

One is that we have at our disposal the psychological insights and tools that Freud and psychotherapy have produced for us over the last hundred years.

And two, we have available the meditation practices of the East that have come to us here in the West over the last century or so. There's a whole inner 'technology' now open to us that we can learn about, draw on, and practise. It's not a theory to learn and understand (although theory is part of it) so much as a set of tools to use for our exploration and journeying.

In this book I'm showing what happens if you take those two sets of tools now available, and put them together with writing poetry. I have my views on what it is that happens, but the important person here is you. Please try the experiment for yourself, and come to your own conclusions.

Vulnerability

Shaping up this kind of poetry is an exercise in vulnerability. When you do it this way you cannot help but be present in your poems in a profoundly personal way. You have been in contact with deeper parts of your being and that contact will manifest in whatever you write. What you write reflects the essence of those moments when you made contact.

It is possible to edit out this vulnerability. You can work and work on the poem, changing this and adding that until the essence of your being is wiped out or overwritten by what is more conventionally acceptable. We could describe this process as re-erecting defences that you can hide your true self behind. There is nothing wrong as such with defences. We need them at times. What is problematic is if we are not aware of our defences and they dominate our being as a matter of habit.

If we deliberately employ our defences to water down our original poem then that is at least a choice. We might need to question why we make that choice, but it is still our choice.

The point about vulnerability is that it is real. We are vulnerable. When we can choose to be vulnerable or not then we are freer than when we have no choice – either because we are not aware there is a choice, or because our defences are so ingrained that we cannot put them down. Think mediaeval knight in armour

173

here: relatively safe from attack, but seriously curtailed in freedom of movement, and quickly exhausted by the effort of carrying around all that metal plate.

When we choose to be vulnerable, to be real, to be our true selves as much as we can, then we have taken our power back to ourselves from those people (the 'bad' guys) in whom we have previously invested it. It is exhilarating and freeing. This freedom and exhilaration will manifest in our poetry when the poem reflects the vulnerability and realness we encounter when we touch the deepness in ourselves. It will energise and reassure anyone who reads it who is looking for that kind of movement and change.

If we choose to conceal our vulnerability, our true selves, behind layers of words, and images, and distorting phrases, then we may feel we have protected our self, but we will have simply added to the construct of our false self and added to the weight on our true self. Our true, vulnerable self will be the poorer and the weaker for it.

Anyone reading poems of this kind who wants to protect and conceal their vulnerability will be reassured, even if they don't like the poem. Anyone who is seeking clues as to how to be more in touch with their true self will be dispirited and leaden, and more or less depressed.

Zen lessons: judgement, or acceptance.

One of the insights from Zen, one that we can usefully apply to our poetry, concerns distinctions and judgements. This insight may well help in dealing both with our internal critics, and any we may come across in the actual outside world.

One of the factors we have to contend with in our inner journey is our relationship with desire on the one hand and aversion on the other. In the relative, everyday world we usually move towards those things we like and away from those things we don't. If we do that in our meditation practice we then spend a lot of time and energy doing the same in our inner world.

If we want to be more aware, have more choice, move beyond the everyday then we need to be aware of our desires and aversions, but not follow them, not be caught up in them, not let them rule our life, both inner and outer. In meditation we can practise letting our desires arise, letting them hang around for a while, and then letting them pass on. We can do the same with our aversions or dislikes. In doing this, in becoming more skillful at it, we gradually learn to recognise things simply as they are. We gradually learn to apprehend Reality simply as it is.

One of the ways we can practise with this in the outer world is by becoming more aware of our judgements. When we decide that something is 'good' or 'bad' we are entering the area of desire and aversion, and we are feeding that habit. We can practise letting the judgements come and go, but not holding on to them. What does our world look like if we do that?

We can apply this insight to our judgements around our own poems and those of other people. When we notice judgements arising (and they will!) we can practise noticing. We can name the process ('Ah, I'm judging now.') and we can let it come and let it go.

When other people make judgements about us or our work, we can do the same practice for them, silently, for our own benefit, and for theirs.

(Or if we want to be confrontational we can tell them to back off and keep their opinionated opinions to themselves. Not recommending it. Just saying it does happen.)

When the question 'Is this any good?' comes up in us, we can instead ask more interesting questions:

What is the essence of this poem? What is this poem saying? What responses does it evoke in me? What does that say about me? What does that say about how I see the world?

In Zen-speak, what is the 'suchness' of this poem? What is the 'thisness' of this poem?

What may be labelled in conventional terms (perfectly correctly) 'no good' may, when looked at in a spirit of acceptance of what is, turn out to be full of insight and wisdom for you in this moment.

Poetry and inner journey

There is a Zen story about Dogen, a thirteenth century Zen master. He was asked 'What is the enlightened mind?'

He replied, 'The enlightened mind is intimate with all things.'

I first heard this story about two years ago from a great Zen teacher called Flint Sparks. I loved it then, and I love it now. Maybe it's my koan.

The relation of this story to shaping up poems in the way that I am recommending is that when you sit with a topic, and feel your way into it, and allow words to shape themselves into a poem around it, you are developing intimacy with that topic. You get a feel for it in your own way (not somebody else's). I notice I've used the phrase 'get a feel for' in the last sentence. 'Intimacy' means a close warm, physical connection. It's like a personal physical relationship with someone. It's feelingful. You can't just understand something intellectually and have an intimate relationship with it. It's more personal than that. It's intimate.

The journey is yours and you have to do every step yourself. Every realisation has to be yours, in your own individual way. Shaping poems in the way I describe can be helpful to this journey because you know that you are developing intimacy with each topic you write about. And in shaping many poems you are developing your capacity for becoming intimate with all things, and with anything.

So, over to you now.

I wish you well with your poem-shaping, with your capacity for intimacy, and with your journey.

Afterword

Thanks for reading this far and I do hope you have found the book enjoyable and useful.

You'll find more poems and information about other books on the holybloke website (holybloke.com). You can become a holybloke follower and receive email alerts when new poems, posts, and books are published. Sign up on the website.

Finally, if you have enjoyed the book and found it helpful, please consider leaving a short review on Amazon. Help other people to learn how to shape up poems from within!

Also available

Pete's first book of poems, ***The Commitment of the Lark: poems for looking deeply*** was welcomed with this review:

'These poems are remarkably refreshing and invigorating. If you are interested in living life to the full, deeply, honestly, out on the open ocean, away from the safe harbour of dogma, then you will find this book very nourishing. Pete Armstrong's writing has an incisive vitality, a warmth, a curiosity, a compassion, humour, a desire to embrace the whole of life's experience including the 'shadow' as well as the numinous (and indeed, to see the numinous within the shadow), exploring a spiritual path that is very much of the here and now, the everyday. If you are interested in Ken Wilber's Integral writings, Buddhism, mystical Christianity, psychology, these poems will surely touch and inspire you.'

The Commitment of the Lark is available from Amazon as a paperback, and also as an e-book for Kindle.

His second book of poems is ***Target Practice: a guidebook of 100 poems for your inner journey***

The poems in Target Practice are travellers' tales from an inner journey. They contain insights, tips on how to travel safely, and on dangers to avoid.

These poems tell of the experiences and insights of exploration, both inner and outer.

They emerge in and through meditation, and the clarity that can come as part of that. Some are like jokes, and should make you laugh, or at least smile.

Target practice is like a guidebook for your journey into your unknown future.

Target Practice is also available as an e-book for Kindle.

Riding into the Storm: returning to face childhood loss and bereavement

As a child Pete Armstrong lost his father twice over: first when his father became paralysed following an accident at work, and finally three years later when his father died.

As an adult he worked to come to terms with his own grief. As a therapist he also worked with others who were grieving. He thought he knew the territory well, but in time he came to feel that the task of finding meaning and understanding might never be finished.

So as an older man he undertook a journey by bike across northern England, visiting places linked to his childhood, in order to see what more he could learn about the nature of grief and healing in the face of childhood loss.

The journey starts in a gale, but it is in returning to face the feelings which have stayed with him from childhood that he encounters the real storm.

To what degree can he find resolution, peace, and reconciliation?

Join him on the journey to find out.